THE RŌM FIELD GUIDE TO

amphibians and reptiles of
ONTARIO

ROSS D. MacCULLOCH

RŌM

M&S

First published in 2002 by the Royal Ontario Museum and McClelland & Stewart Ltd.

A ROM Science Publication

Project Director: Glen Ellis

Manuscript Editor for ROM Sciences Editorial Board:
    Richard Winterbottom

Publication Editors: Glen Ellis, Andrea Gallagher, Alex Schultz

Designer (Interior): Virginia Morin

Designer (Cover): Tara Winterhalt

Production Manager: Victoria Black

National Library of Canada Cataloguing-in-Publication Data

MacCulloch, Ross Douglas
    The ROM field guide to amphibians and reptiles of Ontario

Co-published by the Royal Ontario Museum.
Includes bibliographical references and index.
ISBN 0-7710-7651-7

1. Amphibians—Ontario—Identification. 2. Reptiles—Ontario—Identification. 3. Amphibians—Ontario. 4. Reptiles—Ontario.
I. Royal Ontario Museum II. Title.

QL654.M33 2002   597.9'09713   C2002-900897-2

The Royal Ontario Museum is an agency of the Ontario Ministry of Tourism, Culture and Recreation.

Royal Ontario Museum   McClelland & Stewart Ltd.
100 Queen's Park   *The Canadian Publishers*
Toronto, Ontario   481 University Avenue
M5S 2C6   Toronto, Ontario
www.rom.on.ca   M5G 2E9
                             www.mcclelland.com

1 2 3 4 5   05 04 03 02

CONTENTS

Introduction 4

Characteristics of Amphibians and Reptiles 5

Amphibians and Reptiles in Ontario 9

Conservation 14

Using this book 16

Further Information on Ontario Amphibians and Reptiles 19

Comparative Photographs 23

Species Accounts: Amphibians of Ontario 33

Salamanders 36

Proteidae / Mudpuppies 37

Salamandridae / Newts and Old World Salamanders 41

Ambystomatidae / Mole Salamanders 45

Plethodontidae / Lungless Salamanders 55

Frogs and Toads 64

Bufonidae / Toads 65

Hylidae / Treefrogs 71

Ranidae / True Frogs 83

Species Accounts: Reptiles of Ontario 97

Turtles 100

Chelydridae / Snapping Turtles 101

Kinosternidae / Musk and Mud Turtles 105

Emydidae / Pond and Marsh Turtles 109

Trionychidae / Softshells 121

Lizards 124

Scincidae / Skinks 125

Snakes 128

Colubridae / Typical Snakes 129

Viperidae / Vipers 159

Glossary 164

Checklist 165

Index 166

Photo Credits 167

Acknowledgments 168

INTRODUCTION

Amphibians and reptiles are an important, although not highly visible, component of our natural systems. They may be surprisingly numerous, even in urban or suburban areas. For example, salamanders may be quite numerous in a stream valley or a ravine, and in some cases they may be the most abundant vertebrate in the area. However, because of their small size, their limited movements, and their habit of burrowing, along with other concealing behaviour, they may go unnoticed. Residents are often surprised to discover that these animals are present in their neighbourhood.

Amphibians and reptiles have limited ability to regulate their body temperature through metabolic means, so they must obtain heat from external sources, principally sun-heated air or ground surfaces. As a result, their activities follow daily, and especially seasonal, cycles. They are most active during spring and summer and are inactive during the cold months.

Amphibians number 4700 species in three groups or orders: salamanders (Caudata); frogs and toads (Anura); and caecilians (Gymnophiona). Caecilians are legless burrowing amphibians found only in the tropics. There are approximately 6000 species of reptiles, distributed in four groups: tuataras (Rhynchocephalia); turtles (Testudines); lizards and snakes (Squamata); and crocodiles (Crocodylia). Tuataras are the last living members of an ancient group of reptiles. They are now found only in New Zealand.

Amphibians and reptiles reach their greatest diversity, or number of species, in the tropics, where they occupy an amazing variety of specialized habitats. Fewer species occur in temperate regions. Ontario is home to 47 species.

CHARACTERISTICS OF
AMPHIBIANS AND REPTILES

Throughout history amphibians and reptiles have been shunned by humans, perhaps because their skins are naked or scaly and they often feel cold to the touch. Even the great biologist Linnaeus referred to them as "foul and loathsome creatures." Fortunately, for every detractor, these animals have had a number of supporters.

AMPHIBIANS

Amphibians evolved from fish-like ancestors about 370 million years ago. Although they can move about on land, they are never completely independent of water. Because their eggs have no shell and are therefore vulnerable to drying, most amphibians must return to water to reproduce. This mode of life—part spent in water and part on land—is the origin of the name "amphibian," formed from the Greek words *amphi* (both) and *bios* (life).

Reproduction

The first warm rains of spring trigger movement in many species—they leave their overwintering sites and move to breeding ponds. At this time many species can be observed at these ponds or crossing roads on their way to a pond. Movement outside the breeding season depends also on precipitation. Amphibians move more readily and travel greater distances on rainy nights than during dry periods.

From breeding ponds, male frogs call to attract females and, in some species, to announce their presence to potential rival males. Many salamander species congregate at the same ponds year after year, finding mates by olfaction (smell). For many amphibians, the spring breeding season is the only time when they may be easily found. In these species the breeding season is short, and once the eggs are deposited, the adults leave the pond and spend the rest of the year away from water, sometimes buried in leaf litter or underground.

The eggs usually hatch after a few weeks, although some species hatch more quickly. After hatching, the larvae, as young amphibians are called, normally spend some time in water, respiring through gills. The larval stage can last from several weeks to several years. It is usually short in those species that deposit their eggs in shallow or temporary ponds, which dry up during the summer. Species requiring a longer larval stage utilize habitats where water is present year-round.

Metamorphosis

Metamorphosis (transformation from larva to adult) involves a number of anatomical changes. Limbs grow and gills shrink as lungs develop. Salamander larvae have the same general body form as the adults, but in frogs the change in body shape from larva (tadpole) to adult is striking. In salamanders the forelegs develop first, but in frog tadpoles, the hindlegs are the first to appear.

In tadpoles the mouth is adapted for scraping algae. During metamorphosis, the mouth becomes broader and the algae-scraping "teeth" are lost. The intestine shortens as the frog's diet changes from herbivorous to carnivorous. Limbs and lungs grow, and the gills and tail are resorbed.

Although newly metamorphosed amphibians have the adult body form, they are properly called juveniles. Once the limbs and lungs are fully developed, juvenile amphibians leave the breeding pond to live on land. At this stage juveniles may travel considerable distances from their place of birth. This movement enables species to colonize new habitat and allows intermingling of gene pools.

Skin

Amphibian skin is permeable to water. Amphibians do not drink water, but rather absorb it through the skin, especially the skin of the belly. They are also susceptible to water loss through the skin. As a result, most amphibians must occupy moist habitats to minimize water loss. Some amphibians, notably toads, have thick glandular skin that reduces water loss; thick-skinned species can utilize drier environments.

Amphibian skin contains glands that produce a variety of substances. Several of these substances, including mucus, limit the amount of water lost by evaporation through the skin and protect against bacterial infection. Some amphibians have a pair of large glands, one on each side behind the head, in the shoulder region, called parotoid glands. These produce a secretion that can be irritating or even toxic to predators. Amphibians shed their skin as they grow and eat it almost immediately.

Diet

All adult amphibians are carnivorous, feeding on insects, worms, slugs, and sometimes other amphibians. Many frogs and some salamanders can protract their tongue to capture prey, even flying insects. The sticky surface of the tongue facilitates prey capture. Prey is swallowed whole; for larger prey, the forelimbs are used to push the food into the mouth. Most tadpoles feed on algae or tiny particles of vegetation suspended in the water. This diet requires a complex digestive system, and in some tadpoles the long, coiled intestine can be seen through the transparent belly skin. Salamander larvae are carnivorous, and some prey on tadpoles and even on larvae of their own species.

Metabolism

Aquatic amphibian larvae use gills to obtain oxygen from water. In salamander larvae the gills are located on the sides of the neck and have a feathery appearance. In tadpoles the gills are internal; the tadpole takes in water through its mouth, passes it across the gills, and expels it from an opening called the spiracle on the side of the body. Adult amphibians are air breathers. Adult frogs do not have ribs, so they cannot inhale by chest expansion. Instead, they push air into their lungs by repeated pulsations of their mouth and throat. Some salamanders, including some of our most familiar species, have no lungs. Lungless salamanders obtain oxygen through their moist skin, especially the lining of the mouth and throat.

Overwintering frogs can obtain oxygen from water through their skin, although oxygen may become scarce in frozen-over ponds as winter progresses. If the water's oxygen content drops to critical levels, frogs and other animals overwintering in the pond may die. This phenomenon is called "winter kill" and is indicated by the presence of dead animals when the ice melts in spring. Frogs also have a limited capacity for anaerobic (without oxygen) metabolism.

Some frog species can adjust their body chemistry to withstand temperatures a few degrees below freezing, although they cannot tolerate such temperatures for extended periods.

REPTILES

Reptiles first appeared some 330 million years ago from a generalized amphibian-like ancestor. There are several important differences between amphibians and reptiles, especially in reproduction, anatomy, and metabolism.

Reproduction

Reptiles do not congregate at ponds to breed but have a number of other strategies for finding a mate. In some species, many individuals congregate in a single location to overwinter. When the animals emerge in the spring, finding a mate is easy. This behaviour of overwintering in a common den or hibernaculum may have evolved from the advantage it confers in early mating or because of a shortage of suitable sites for hibernation.

Although some snake species bear live young, most of Ontario's reptiles reproduce by laying eggs. Incubation time depends on the temperature of the nest. Turtles dig holes and bury their eggs, while snakes and lizards deposit them in leaf litter or decaying logs. In some snake species the female guards the eggs and may coil around them to protect and even warm them slightly.

Eggs

The reptile egg is very different from the amphibian egg in that it is protected by a shell that helps to retain the egg's internal moisture and nutrients. Reptiles therefore do not have to lay their eggs in water, although they usually choose a moist location. Indeed, reptile eggs cannot be deposited in water; even sea turtles, which spend their entire lives in water, must leave the sea to lay their eggs on land. The shell of most reptile eggs is leathery and flexible. Reptile eggs are similar in structure to bird eggs; this is not surprising—birds evolved from reptile ancestors and therefore are, technically, reptiles.

In reptiles there is no larval stage; the newly hatched young resemble small adults. Young reptiles may travel considerable distances searching for food and a place to spend the winter. Juveniles may return to the same overwintering location used by their parents, or they may find a different site. Such travel allows the reptiles to invade new habitats and to mix gene pools.

Skin

The skin of reptiles is impervious to water, thus preventing water loss through the skin and allowing them to function independently of water. Their impervious skin also permits some reptiles, such as sea turtles and sea snakes, to live in a saltwater environment. No amphibians can live in marine habitats. These characteristics of skin and egg, both affecting the animals' water balance, have allowed reptiles to flourish in habitats such as deserts, which are much less suitable for amphibians.

Diet

Most reptiles are carnivorous, although a few large lizards and turtles are herbivorous. Some freshwater turtles consume aquatic vegetation either deliberately or while foraging for the animals that live in the vegetation. Reptiles typically consume a variety of invertebrates such as insects, worms, crustaceans, and molluscs, but a number of reptile species feed on vertebrates such as fish, amphibians, rodents, and other reptiles. Some species are scavengers, some forage actively for prey, and some use the "sit and wait" strategy, remaining motionless, often concealed or camouflaged, until a suitable prey animal appears. Reptile teeth are not suited for chewing, so food is swallowed whole or torn apart. Smaller prey are easily handled whole, but larger prey are usually killed before being eaten. Many snakes use either constriction or venom to kill their prey. The rate of a reptile's growth depends on the amount of food it consumes. Many reptiles shed their skins as they grow; unlike amphibians, they do not eat the shed skin.

Metabolism

Most reptile species overwinter underground, buried in the soil or in rock formations that allow the animals to descend below the frost line. Turtles overwintering at the bottom of ponds, rivers, or lakes, have reduced metabolic rates and oxygen requirements because of the cold water and diminished activity. During this time, their metabolism functions anaerobically (without oxygen). The turtles can, however, obtain some oxygen from the water through the lining of the mouth and cloaca. When the water warms in spring, they surface and resume normal metabolism.

Some turtle species can tolerate temperatures a few degrees below freezing, but only for short periods.

AMPHIBIANS AND REPTILES IN ONTARIO

Because of its location and size, extending from Lake Erie in the south to Hudson Bay in the north, Ontario has the greatest amphibian and reptile diversity of any Canadian province: 23 amphibian and 24 reptile species.

Generally, distributions of amphibians and reptiles depend on the availability of suitable habitat. By combining our knowledge of geology with the distributions of plants and animals, it is possible to reconstruct the patterns by which plants and animals moved northward after the end of the last Ice Age. At their peak, about 20,000 years ago, glaciers covered all of Ontario. As the ice retreated, our present flora and fauna expanded their ranges northward, and as the climate stabilized, plant and animal communities became established. Although these communities changed slowly under natural conditions, human activity has accelerated the rate of change in species distributions. Land used for housing, industry, and agriculture is unsuitable for most wildlife.

THE CHALLENGE OF CLIMATE

Ontario's climate poses a number of challenges to its amphibians and reptiles. Although winter may be long and cold, summer is the most critical, because during this short time species must reproduce, grow, and store up sufficient reserves of energy to enable them to survive through winter.

Winter

Their metabolism slowed by lower temperatures, amphibians and reptiles must overwinter in places where they can avoid the most extreme cold and where their reduced mobility will not make them vulnerable to predation.

Some frogs and salamanders bury themselves in the soil, sometimes to a depth of at least a metre in the southern part of the province. Other frog species, as well as most turtles, spend the winter at the bottom of a body of water. Snakes usually congregate in a favourable spot, called a den or hibernaculum, for overwintering.

Hibernacula

Snakes return to the hibernaculum in autumn as the days get shorter. Typical hibernacula are in rock formations that offer relatively easy access through fissures and crevices to refuges below the frost line. Some hibernacula are used by many individuals of more than one species. Common Gartersnakes in particular are known for congregating in large numbers at suitable hibernacula. Although the great densities of snakes found in Manitoba have not been seen in Ontario, the number of individuals and species that share a den may be considerable.

Snakes usually return to the same den year after year, but as human numbers increase, new housing, industrial, and commercial developments may be built over traditional hibernacula. When a snake hibernaculum is destroyed, the returning snakes cannot find their traditional wintering site, and they search for new places to overwinter. They explore buildings, excavations, and other human constructions in search of a new refuge.

To a snake, a cracked foundation or a broken basement window offers sanctuary from the coming cold. Homeowners may be understandably alarmed by the arrival of a large number of snakes in their house. There is no chemical repellent that is effective against snakes and not harmful to humans. Snakes must therefore be physically prevented from entering where they are not wanted. For homes in rural areas or near known hibernacula, an annual inspection of the foundation is prudent. Sometimes snakes enter a basement and pass the winter there unnoticed until they emerge in the spring. At this time, their point of exit can be determined and, once the snakes have all departed, it can be sealed off to prevent their return. Abandoned buildings or unused basements can become established hibernacula. Purchasers of older buildings may be surprised to learn that they are sharing their new property with a den of snakes.

Spring

Activity begins again when temperatures rise in spring. Since air temperature increases more rapidly than water temperature, species that spend the winter at the bottom of ponds or other water bodies emerge later than species that overwinter on land. All energy is concentrated on reproduction—most species do not begin to feed until breeding has been completed. The earlier the breeding, the earlier the birth of the new generation, and the greater the amount of time for the young animals to grow and store energy for winter.

Frogs and salamanders head for breeding ponds. Some species enter ponds to breed even before the ice has completely disappeared. These are species that breed in temporary ponds, which dry up during the summer. In order to produce a new generation, they must breed early, so that the juveniles will be able to mature soon enough to be able to leave the pond before it dries. Species that occur the farthest north, where the summer is shortest, are also early breeders.

When reptiles emerge from their winter dens, they immediately begin searching for a mate. Most reptiles lay eggs. The speed of embryonic development in the egg depends on the temperature of the location where the eggs are laid. A viviparous (live-bearing) female snake, however, can seek out a warm location and incubate her growing young more rapidly, affording the newborns more time to prepare for winter. Live-bearing species, such as Common Gartersnakes, can reproduce successfully in a very short summer and consequently are found much farther north than egg-laying species.

Summer and Autumn

Early breeding is critical in Ontario's short summers for those species that produce a new generation in a single year. However, some amphibians, such as the American Bullfrog and Green Frog, breed over an extended period in midsummer. Unlike early breeders, the tadpoles of these frogs spend one or more winters in the water before transforming. For these species, the short summer is not as limiting as it is for early breeders, but they can only inhabit water that is deep enough not to dry up in summer or freeze to the bottom in winter.

Turtles bury their eggs in the soil, usually in sunny locations, where the warm soil accelerates development. Most species hatch in late summer, leaving the young turtles only a few weeks to prepare for the coming winter. They must feed and store enough fat reserves to nourish themselves until spring. In some species, notably the Painted Turtle, the young may remain in the nest through the winter, using their egg yolk for nourishment and emerging the following spring. These young turtles can withstand below-freezing temperatures in their shallow nests.

OBSERVING AMPHIBIANS AND REPTILES

Salamanders often conceal themselves in damp soil in wooded areas. They may be found by turning over logs or stones in these locations. It is important to replace the log or stone afterwards to minimize disturbance to the habitat.

Turtles raise their body temperature by basking in sunshine, out of water. Midmorning until early afternoon are the best times to observe basking. Turtles bask less frequently later in the day and also bask less as summer progresses. Young turtles are seen less often, perhaps because they feed in shallow water, which is fairly warm, and therefore do not need to bask out of water. Female turtles may also be observed away from water, searching for a spot to lay their eggs. Many turtles deposit their eggs in the same area, usually year after year. Predators such as raccoons search for and dig up the nests, and eat the eggs. A nest, providing it is not discovered by predators, may be monitored until late summer when, in most species, the young turtles emerge. After hatching, they head for water, where they forage among vegetation in shallow areas, usually near the water's edge.

Snakes and lizards are best observed while they are basking or foraging for food. They usually bask from midmorning to early afternoon and forage in the habitat of their preferred prey. Snakes and lizards may often be found under logs or discarded boards, where they like to hide.

IDENTIFICATION

Appearance

Observation of size, shape, and colour is the obvious first step in determining identification. Few turtle species grow larger than 25 cm (10") in shell length. Some turtles have a high, domed, somewhat elongate shell, while in others the shell is flatter and less elongate. Most of the smaller snake species never exceed 50 cm (20") in length, and only a few species grow to one metre. Some snakes are blotched, some have longitudinal stripes, and some are unicoloured. Similarly, some frogs are unicoloured, some are spotted, and some have two prominent light-coloured stripes down the back.

Habitat

Habitat can be a useful tool for identifying species. Small frogs such as Spring Peepers, for instance, will not be found in large lakes, and bullfrogs are unlikely to be encountered in small forest ponds. Woodland ponds are home to breeding mole salamanders and their larvae, while Northern Two-lined Salamanders breed in streams, and Eastern Red-backed Salamanders never enter water. Map Turtles occur only in large bodies of water, while Painted Turtles prefer smaller ponds.

Identification of larval amphibians can be very difficult, even for experts. Several species of mole salamanders (family Ambystomatidae) may breed in the same pond, and the larvae are difficult to distinguish. Among frogs, differentiating between tadpoles of American and Fowler's toads, Leopard and Pickerel frogs, and Green and Mink frogs is especially difficult. Some species may be eliminated because of location or habitat, but often a pond must be revisited, after the larvae have begun to transform, in order to confirm identification.

Season

Time of year can be another useful tool in identification of tadpoles or larvae. Most species complete their larval period in one summer, so tadpoles of these species will not be present in early spring or fall. Large spring or fall tadpoles can belong only to those species that spend a winter in the larval stage (American Bullfrog, Green Frog, and Mink Frog). These species are also restricted to larger bodies of water—those that do not dry up during summer or freeze to the bottom in winter.

During the breeding season, in spring or early summer, frogs can be located by following the mating calls of the males. Salamanders do not call, but those species that breed in ponds, bogs, or streams may also be observed there in the spring.

Adding to the Understanding

Any observer interested in amphibians and reptiles can make a contribution to the understanding of their biology. Of primary importance is the distribution of the species—where are they found? In what microhabitat? At what time of day or year? In what weather conditions? By combining these basic pieces of information, a better picture of the ecology of our amphibians and reptiles can be developed. Much of the data in the distribution maps in this book were contributed by interested naturalists.

Anyone who wishes to contribute distribution information should contact the Natural Heritage Information Centre, Ontario Ministry of Natural Resources, at the Web site listed on page 20. In such cases it is important that the identification of the species can be confirmed. A good photograph of the specimen is necessary to prove identification and to validate the sighting.

A number of organizations conduct amphibian surveys and many of them need volunteers to monitor the presence of amphibians in their neighbourhood and to report to a central data bank. In Ontario the organization is Frogwatch Ontario. Nationally, the Environmental Monitoring and Assessment Network monitors populations of amphibians and reptiles. The Web sites for these two organizations are listed on page 20.

Many regional naturalists' societies conduct nature walks and field trips that include observing amphibians and reptiles. Some of these organizations are listed on page 21. Chances are good that there is such an organization in your area.

CONSERVATION

As humans steadily encroach upon the natural world, preservation of our biodiversity becomes more critical. Setting aside large tracts of land as undisturbed habitat for wildlife is important, but conservation on a smaller scale is also effective. Small woodlots or wetlands interspersed among subdivisions or separated by highways—even an uncultivated area of a backyard—can provide habitat for amphibians and reptiles as well as for a number of insects, other invertebrates, and native plants.

Many amphibians and reptiles fall victim to road traffic, while others are deliberately killed by humans who find them distasteful or frightening. Many species of snake, not only rattlesnakes, vibrate their tail tip if excited. If the tail comes into contact with dry fallen leaves, a sound similar to that of a rattlesnake may be produced. Many harmless snakes are killed because this behaviour causes people to mistake them for rattlesnakes.

Legal Issues

In Ontario, amphibians and reptiles, like other wildlife, are under the jurisdiction of the Ministry of Natural Resources. With certain exceptions, it is unlawful to keep in captivity, displace, or otherwise disturb any amphibian or reptile. Exceptions may be made for educational purposes, allowing some species to be kept in captivity. The Snapping Turtle and the American Bullfrog may be hunted, and these two species fall under the angling regulations of the Ministry of Natural Resources. All inquiries regarding protection of amphibians and reptiles should be directed to the Ministry of Natural Resources. Many other provinces have similar legislation.

Amphibians and Reptiles as Pets

Because of their exotic appearance, amphibians and reptiles are popular pets. Prospective owners of such pets must, however, keep in mind that, as noted above, it is in most cases illegal to possess native amphibians and reptiles in Ontario and in many other jurisdictions. Remember also that many amphibians and reptiles have very precise habitat requirements. It is often difficult to duplicate the necessary microhabitat in a home terrarium. As a result, despite the best of intentions, the captive animal may not survive.

Many amphibians and reptiles offered for sale in pet shops have been wild-caught in other countries. Although sale of these animals may be legal, and although they may be well treated in the pet shop, the animals are often poorly treated en route, and many die before reaching the vendor. Collecting from the wild can also have a detrimental effect on natural populations.

Many species, especially reptiles, have a long lifespan. That cute baby turtle can live for up to 30 years, requiring increasingly larger containers and needing frequent cleaning. Also, youthful enthusiasm for keeping a pet may dwindle with time, resulting in an unwanted animal that requires considerable maintenance. Often a pet that has grown too large or is no longer wanted is "dumped" in the wild, where it usually perishes.

Anyone considering keeping an amphibian or reptile as a pet must understand that this can be a long-term commitment, depending on the lifespan of the species. Also, prospective petkeepers should ensure that their pet was bred in captivity, to minimize damage to wild populations and to maximize the likelihood that the animal will do well in captivity.

Amphibian Populations in Decline?

Recent research has served to focus attention on the question of declining amphibian, particularly frog, populations. One of the leading causes of this is disturbance and destruction of habitat. In the tropics, where an amphibian species may occur only in one small area, habitat disturbance may easily result in the extinction of the species. In Ontario most of our amphibian species are more widely distributed, making them less susceptible to extinction, but cases of local, provincial, and even national extirpation are well documented.

Amphibians, however, have shown themselves to be remarkably resilient. Longer-term studies of amphibian populations show that some ponds whose populations had declined drastically have rebounded within a few years, with population sizes restored to their pre-decline numbers. Because of the large numbers of eggs that a single female can produce, amphibians have the potential for rapid population growth. In fact, some ponds that had no amphibians for several years have been recolonized by the arrival of a few juveniles dispersing from other ponds.

USING THIS BOOK

COMPARATIVE PHOTOGRAPHS

Users of this guide should consult the section on Comparative Photographs on pages 24–32 as a first step in identifying an unknown species. In this section photographs of similar species are placed on the same page to facilitate identification by comparison. The photographs have been chosen to show characters that are useful in identification. Each species photograph is accompanied by a map showing the distribution in Ontario.

SPECIES ACCOUNTS

Taxonomy assigns names and classifications to living things. Each species has a two-word scientific name composed of genus (plural: genera) and species. The scientific name is usually italicized, and the first name begins with a capital letter. For example, the Wood Frog, *Rana sylvatica,* belongs to the genus *Rana* and has the specific name *sylvatica.* The genus name *Rana* (Latin for frog) shows that it is related to other frogs in the same genus, such as bullfrogs and Leopard Frogs. The specific name, in this case, *sylvatica,* meaning "of the forest," is unique for each species. This system provides internationally accepted names that are much more stable than common names, which may have many local variants. In this book both scientific and common names follow the convention established by the Society for the Study of Amphibians and Reptiles (Crother et al., 2000).

   Classification involves a hierarchical ranking system. A family consists of one or more genera, an order contains one or more families, and a class may contain several orders.

   In this guide, amphibians and reptiles are grouped into families, such as the Ranidae (true frogs), and orders such as the Anura (frogs and toads). All amphibians are in the class Amphibia, and reptiles are in the class Reptilia.

   Two pages are devoted to each species. The numbers below the name show the maximum size of the species: total length for salamanders and lizards, head + body length for frogs, and shell length for turtles. Note that these are maximum reported sizes; most individuals will be smaller.

   The section entitled "Appearance" contains the physical description of the species. The text indicated by an arrow (▶) points out how the species differs from similar species with which it might be confused. The subsequent section, "Habitat and Behaviour," details characteristics that may aid in finding the species in the wild. "Reproduction" provides information on the reproductive aspects of the species' biology.

   The status of each species of amphibian and reptile in Ontario is evaluated by two organizations: the Committee on the Status of Endangered Wildlife in Canada (COSEWIC), and the Ontario Ministry of Natural Resources (OMNR).

COSEWIC uses the following status categories:

not at risk—a species that has been evaluated and found to be not at risk.

indeterminate—a species for which there is insufficient information to support a status designation.

vulnerable or **special concern**—a species of special concern because of characteristics that make it particularly sensitive to human activities or natural events, but does not include an extirpated, endangered, or threatened species.

threatened—a species likely to become endangered if nothing is done to reverse the factors leading to its extirpation or extinction.

endangered—a species facing imminent extirpation or extinction throughout its range.

extirpated—a species no longer existing in the wild in Canada, but occurring elsewhere in the wild.

extinct—a species that no longer exists.

OMNR uses the following status categories:

vulnerable—of special concern in Ontario but not yet threatened or endangered.

threatened—at risk of becoming endangered.

endangered—at risk of becoming extirpated or extinct.

extirpated—no longer present in Ontario, but occurring elsewhere.

extinct—no longer present anywhere on Earth.

The COSEWIC and OMNR status for each species is provided in the "Status" section of each account. The status of Ontario species is periodically updated on the Royal Ontario Museum Web site, www.rom.on.ca/ontario/

DISTRIBUTION MAPS

The distributions of each species in Ontario and North America are shown on maps. The Ontario maps reflect the distributions as determined by the Ontario Herpetofaunal Summaries, a series of surveys of the province's herpetofauna involving dozens of contributors. These maps are not necessarily complete; they represent only the information available to date. Many species of amphibians and reptiles are at the northern limits of their range in Ontario, and these limits are often not well defined.

Species distributions may be limited by length of the active season or availability of habitat, be it suitable vegetation, water body type, or overwintering sites. Habitat requirements are complex and varied, and not fully understood. A species may be absent from a seemingly suitable habitat because an important component, not obvious to a human observer, is missing. Furthermore, distributions change over time, so repeated observations from the same location are especially valuable.

Species Distribution in Ontario and North America

The coloured areas show the known ranges of each species. Any and all subspecies are included in the range. We must keep in mind, however, that a species will not be uniformly distributed across the range shown on the maps. Each species will be restricted to the appropriate habitat within its range. More detailed distribution maps are available on the Web site of the Natural Heritage Information Centre, Ontario Ministry of Natural Resources (see page 20).

The maps may be useful in identifying an unknown species by eliminating possibilities that do not occur in your location. For example, species that occur only on Pelee Island in Lake Erie will not be found in central Ontario.

An abbreviated version of this guide can be found on the Royal Ontario Museum Web site, www.rom.on.ca/ontario/

FURTHER INFORMATION ON ONTARIO AMPHIBIANS AND REPTILES

BOOKS AND OTHER PRINT SOURCES

Bishop, C. A., and K. E. Pettit, eds. 1991. *Declines in Canadian Amphibian Populations: Designing a National Monitoring Strategy.* Canadian Wildlife Service Occasional Paper No. 76, Ottawa, ON.

Conant, R., and J. T. Collins. 1998. *A Field Guide to Reptiles and Amphibians of Eastern and Central North America.* 3rd ed. (Peterson Series). Houghton Mifflin, Boston, MA.

Cook, F. R. 1984. *Introduction to Canadian Amphibians and Reptiles.* National Museum of Natural Sciences, National Museums of Canada, Ottawa, ON.

Crother, B. I., chair. 2000. *Scientific and Standard English Names of Amphibians and Reptiles of North America North of Mexico, with Comments Regarding Confidence in Our Understanding.* Herpetological Circular No. 29. Society for the Study of Amphibians and Reptiles, Lawrence, KS.

Green, D. M., ed. 1997. *Amphibians in Decline.* Reports from the Canadian Declining Amphibian Populations Task Force. Herpetological Conservation 1, Herpetologists' League.

Harding, J. H. 1997. *Amphibians and Reptiles of the Great Lakes Region.* University of Michigan Press, Lansing, MI.

Johnson, B. 1989. *Familiar Amphibians and Reptiles of Ontario.* Natural Heritage/Natural History Inc., Toronto, ON.

Moriarty, J., and A. M. Bauer. 2000. State and Provincial Amphibians and Reptiles Publications for the United States and Canada. Herpetological Circular No. 28. Society for the Study of Amphibians and Reptiles, Lawrence, KS.

Powell, R., J. T. Collins, and E. D. Hooper. 1998. *A Key to Amphibians and Reptiles of the Continental United States and Canada.* University Press of Kansas, Lawrence, KS.

Preston, W. B. 1982. *The Amphibians and Reptiles of Manitoba.* Manitoba Museum of Man and Nature, Winnipeg, MB.

Russell, A. P., and A. M. Bauer. 2000. *The Amphibians and Reptiles of Alberta: A Field Guide and Primer of Boreal Herpetology.* 2nd ed. University of Calgary Press, Calgary, AB.

Tyning, T. F. 1990. *A Guide to Amphibians and Reptiles* (Stokes Nature Series). Little, Brown and Company, Boston, MA.

Weller, W. F., and M. J. Oldham, eds. 1988. *Ontario Herpetofaunal Summary 1986.* Ontario Field Herpetologists, Peterborough, ON.

Zim, H. S., J. G. Irving, and H. M. Smith. 2001. *Reptiles and Amphibians* (Golden Guide). Golden Press, New York, NY.

INTERNET SOURCES

Provincial and National Parks in Ontario

Information on the herpetofauna of Ontario provincial parks, counties, and regions, and on national parks in Ontario, may be found on the Web sites of the Ontario Ministry of Natural Resources, Environment Canada, Parks Canada, and Ontario Provincial Parks, listed below. Many print publications are also available from these sources.

Environment Canada
www.ec.gc.ca
Ontario Region
www.on.ec.gc.ca/wildlife/intro.html
Species at Risk
www.speciesatrisk.gc.ca

Ontario Ministry of Natural Resources
www.mnr.gov.on.ca/MNR
Natural Heritage Information Centre
www.mnr.gov.on.ca/MNR/nhic
Detailed distribution maps of Ontario amphibians and reptiles
www.mnr.gov.on.ca/MNR/nhic/herps/ohs.html
List of vulnerable, threatened, endangered, extirpated,
or extinct species of Ontario
www.mnr.gov.on.ca/mnr/vteeelist_2001

Ontario Provincial Parks
www.ontarioparks.com

Parks Canada Species at Risk Program
www.parkscanada.gc.ca

Other Agencies and Organizations

American Society of Ichthyologists and Herpetologists
www.utexas.edu/depts/asih

Canadian Amphibian and Reptile Conservation Network
www.carcnet.ca

Canadian Museum of Nature
www.mus-nature.ca

Committee on the Status of Endangered Wildlife in Canada (COSEWIC)
www.cosewic.gc.ca/cosewic

Eastern Massasauga Rattlesnake Recovery Team
www.terra-plex.com/SIN

Environmental Monitoring and Assessment Network
www.eman-rese.ca/emanops/intro

Frogwatch Ontario
www.cciw.ca/frogwatching

Herpetologists' League
www.inhs.uiuc.edu/cbd/HL/HL.html

Royal Ontario Museum
www.rom.on.ca
Centre for Biodiversity and Conservation Biology
www.rom.on.ca/biodiversity/cbcb
Online Field Guides and Species at Risk
www.rom.on.ca/ontario/

Society for the Study of Amphibians and Reptiles
www.ku.edu/~ssar

Toronto Zoo Adopt-a-pond Program
www.torontozoo.com/adoptapond

Ontario Natural History Societies

The following list of Ontario natural history societies is by no means
exhaustive. Those whose Web sites are listed below have an interest in
amphibians and reptiles and in some cases are a source of information.

Essex County Field Naturalists
www.city.windsor.on.ca/ojibway/ECFN.htm

Federation of Ontario Naturalists
www.ontarionature.org

Georgian Bay Reptile Awareness Program
www.gbayreptiles.com

Hamilton Naturalists' Club
www.freenet.hamilton.on.ca/link/hamnature/

Kingston Field Naturalists
http://psyc.queensu.ca/~davids/kfn.html

McIlwraith Field Naturalists
http://info.london.on.ca/environment/mfn

Norfolk Field Naturalists
www.kwic.com/~nfn/

Ottawa Field-Naturalists' Club
www.achilles.net/ofnc

Thunder Bay Field Naturalists
www.tbfn.bay.net

Toronto Field Naturalists
www.sources.com/tfn/

Woodstock Field Naturalists
www.execulink.com/~wfnc/

COMPARATIVE
PHOTOGRAPHS

COMPARISON OF
THE AMPHIBIANS OF ONTARIO

Salamanders

Mudpuppy
Necturus maculosus
Species account, p. 38

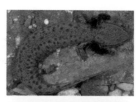

Eastern Newt
Notophthalmus viridescens
Adult
Species account, p. 42

Eastern Newt
Notophthalmus viridescens
Juvenile (eft)
Species account, p. 42

Blue-spotted Salamander
Ambystoma laterale
Species account, p. 46

Jefferson Salamander
Ambystoma jeffersonianum
Species account, p. 48

Small-mouthed Salamander
Ambystoma texanum
Species account, p. 50

Salamanders

Spotted Salamander
Ambystoma maculatum
Species account, p. 52

Northern Dusky Salamander
Desmognathus fuscus
Species account, p. 56

Northern Two-lined
Salamander
Eurycea bislineata
Species account, p. 58

Four-toed Salamander
Hemidactylium scutatum
Species account, p. 60

Eastern Red-backed
Salamander
Plethodon cinereus
Species account, p. 62

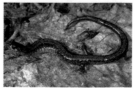

Frogs and Toads

American Toad
Bufo americanus
Species account, p. 66

Fowler's Toad
Bufo fowleri
Species account, p. 68

Gray Treefrog
Hyla versicolor
Species account, p. 72

Northern Cricket Frog
Acris crepitans
Species account, p. 74

Spring Peeper
Pseudacris crucifer
Species account, p. 76

Western Chorus Frog
Pseudacris triseriata
Species account, p. 78

Boreal Chorus Frog
Psuedacris maculata
Species account, p. 80

Frogs and Toads

Wood Frog
Rana sylvatica
Species account, p. 84

Northern Leopard Frog
Rana pipiens
Species account, p. 86

Pickerel Frog
Rana palustris
Species account, p. 88

Green Frog
Rana clamitans
Species account, p. 90

Mink Frog
Rana septentrionalis
Species account, p. 92

American Bullfrog
Rana catesbeiana
Species account, p. 94

COMPARISON OF THE REPTILES OF ONTARIO

Turtles

Snapping Turtle
Chelydra serpentina
Species account, p. 102

Stinkpot
Sternotherus odoratus
Species account, p. 106

Painted Turtle
Chrysemys picta
Species account, p. 110

Northern Map Turtle
Graptemys geographica
Species account, p. 112

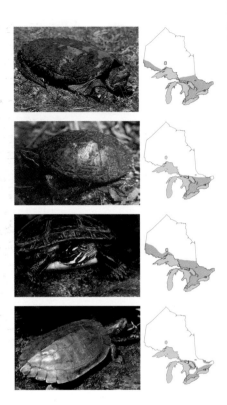

Turtles

Blanding's Turtle
Emydoidea blandingii
Species account, p. 114

Spotted Turtle
Clemmys guttata
Species account, p. 116

Wood Turtle
Clemmys insculpta
Species account, p. 118

Spiny Softshell
Apalone spinifera
Species account, p. 122

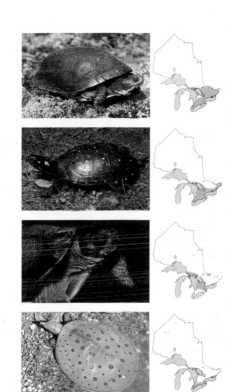

Longitudinally Striped Snakes

Common Gartersnake
Thamnophis sirtalis
Species account, p. 130

Eastern Ribbonsnake
Thamnophis sauritus
Species account, p. 132

Butler's Gartersnake
Thamnophis butleri
Species account, p. 134

Queen Snake
Regina septemvittata
Species account, p. 138

Uniformly Coloured Snakes

Common Gartersnake
Thamnophis sirtalis
(Black Colour Phase)
Species account, p. 130

Eastern Ratsnake
Elaphe obsoleta
Species account, p. 154

Note: Juveniles of this species may
have a blotched pattern.

DeKay's Brownsnake
Storeria dekayi
Species account, p. 140

Red-bellied Snake
Storeria occipitomaculata
Species account, p. 142

Smooth Greensnake
Opheodrys vernalis
Species account, p. 144

Ring-necked Snake
Diadophis punctatus
Species account, p. 146

Eastern Racer
Coluber constrictor
Species account, p. 156

Note: Juveniles of this species may
have a blotched pattern.

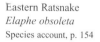

Blotched or Banded Snakes

Northern Watersnake
Nerodia sipedon
Species account, p. 136

Eastern Hog-nosed Snake
Heterodon platirhinos
Species account, p. 148

Milksnake
Lampropeltis triangulum
Species account, p. 150

Eastern Foxsnake
Elaphe gloydi
Species account, p. 152

Massasauga
Sistrurus catenatus
Species account, p. 160

SPECIES ACCOUNTS
AMPHIBIANS OF ONTARIO

In Ontario, amphibians are represented by salamanders (10 species), and frogs and toads (13 species). Salamanders are less diverse than frogs, there being only about 350 species worldwide, compared to about 3500 species of frogs. The greatest number of salamander species is found in eastern North America, in the Appalachian Mountains.

Salamanders

Many salamanders follow the typical amphibian mode of depositing eggs in water, followed by an aquatic larval stage and adults that may be aquatic or terrestrial. Those species that reproduce in ponds usually attach their eggs to submerged objects such as waterlogged branches. Stream breeders typically deposit eggs under stones.

Some species in the family Plethodontidae, however, deposit their eggs out of water, in a moist location. The larval stage takes place inside the egg and the hatchlings resemble adults but are much smaller. The only species in Ontario that follows this pattern of reproduction is the Eastern Red-backed Salamander.

Those species that deposit eggs in water have aquatic larvae that use gills for respiration. The gills are external and are located on the sides of the neck; frog tadpoles have internal gills. Other than the gills, and a fin on the tail, salamander larvae resemble smaller versions of the adults.

Salamanders have a superficial resemblance to lizards, although the differences are obvious on closer examination. Salamanders, like all amphibians, have smooth, moist, scaleless skin and no claws. Lizards have dry scaly skin and claws on their toes. Most salamanders also have a series of grooves, called costal grooves, along the sides of their body, corresponding to the ribs. These grooves are not present in lizards.

The 10 species of salamanders in Ontario are in four families. Two of these families are represented in Ontario by only one species each: the Mudpuppy is the lone representative of the family Proteidae, and the Eastern Newt is the sole member of the Salamandridae. The other families, the mole salamanders and lungless salamanders, are each represented by four species in Ontario.

Frogs and Toads

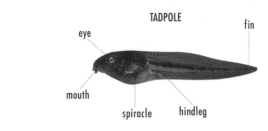

TADPOLE

eye

fin

mouth

spiracle

hindleg

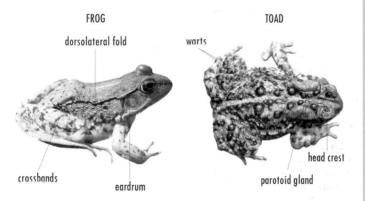

FROG

dorsolateral fold

crossbands

eardrum

TOAD

warts

head crest

parotoid gland

The greatest diversity (number of species) of frogs occurs in tropical forests, especially in Africa, Asia, and South America. Most frogs deposit their eggs in water, and have a free-swimming tadpole stage before metamorphosis.

Although they evolved from salamander-like ancestors, frogs do not have the ancestral amphibian form of an elongate body and tail and short legs. The large head, shortened body, absence of a tail, and long hindlegs indicate a highly specialized anatomy. Frogs also have specialized structures for vocalization, hearing, and prey capture.

Frogs feed on insects, worms, or other invertebrates. Occasionally smaller frogs are eaten by larger frogs, even of the same species. The prey is swallowed whole and is sometimes captured by extending the sticky tongue. The forefeet may be used to push large prey into the mouth.

Thirteen species of frogs are found in Ontario. These belong to three families; toads (2 species), treefrogs (5 species), and true frogs (6 species). All have the typical egg-in-water, tadpole, and adult life cycle.

SALAMANDERS

PROTEIDAE
Mudpuppies

The Proteidae is a small family of salamanders containing only one species in Europe and five species in North America. Members of this family do not leave water upon transformation to adults but are totally aquatic throughout life, retaining their external gills. The Mudpuppy (*Necturus maculosus*) is the only member of this family found in Ontario. Mudpuppies are typically large and are usually the largest salamanders within their range.

MUDPUPPY *Necturus maculosus*

48 cm / 19"

The Mudpuppy is the largest species of salamander found in Canada. Members of this species are rarely encountered because they seldom venture out of their deep-water habitat. They are easily identified by their large size and prominent external gills.

APPEARANCE: The head is flattened, the eyes small, and there are distinctive feathery gills on the side of the head that are retained throughout life (upper photo). The legs are relatively short and the tail is laterally flattened with a small fin on the upper and lower edges. Adults are brown or grey with darker blotches on the back and sides (middle photo). The belly is usually somewhat lighter. Juveniles are more brightly coloured and have yellow stripes that fade with age (lower photo). Newly hatched juveniles are 25 mm (1") in length.

▶ The Mudpuppy is one of only two Ontario salamander species with four toes on the hindfoot; the other is the Four-toed Salamander. Mudpuppies are aquatic throughout life and have obvious external gills (see Comparative Photographs, pp. 24–25).

HABITAT AND BEHAVIOUR: Mudpuppies are usually found at the bottom of rivers and lakes or other large bodies of water. When not foraging for food, they spend most of their time sheltered under submerged objects. They feed on crayfish, aquatic invertebrates, fish eggs, and small fish. They are sometimes caught by anglers, especially in winter.

REPRODUCTION: Eggs are laid in cavities under submerged rocks or logs in May or June. The female guards the eggs until hatching and may remain with the young for a short time after hatching. Mudpuppies reach maturity after about five years.

STATUS: COSEWIC: Not at risk. OMNR: Not at risk.

SALAMANDRIDAE
Newts and Old World Salamanders

This family contains 45 species, most of which are found in Europe and Asia. Six species occur in North America, but only one, the Eastern Newt (*Notophthalmus viridescens*), is found in Ontario. Although adult Salamandridae have no gills, they are usually more aquatic that adults of most other salamander families. Members of this family can be identified by their lack of costal grooves. Newts are fairly distinctive in appearance and are not easily confused with other salamanders.

EASTERN NEWT *Notophthalmus viridescens*

14 cm / 6"

This species is most familiar because of the brightly coloured juvenile newts, or efts, which are often encountered in woodland habitat. The life cycle of newts differs from that of other Ontario salamanders in that the adults return to water after a terrestrial juvenile stage.

APPEARANCE: Adult Eastern Newts are green or yellowish-green with small black spots and two rows of larger red spots along the back (upper photo). Newts from west of Lake Superior have darker backs and few spots. A fin is present on the tail; in males the fin is quite prominent but it is less obvious in females. Efts are seen more frequently than adults. They are usually bright orange with red spots outlined in black on the back (middle photo), although some are less strikingly coloured, light brown or pale orange. The larvae have external gills, a golden tinge, and a black bar through the eye (lower photo).
   ► The brightly coloured efts are unmistakable. Adults can be distinguished by their green background colour with red spots along the back (see Comparative Photographs, pp. 24–25).

HABITAT AND BEHAVIOUR: Adult Eastern Newts are almost completely aquatic and prefer slow-moving water where vegetation is plentiful, especially where the banks are wooded. Eastern Newts feed on insects and other invertebrates. Adults may overwinter at the bottom of the pond or leave water and spend the winter buried in the soil. The efts are found on moist forest floors and seldom enter water. Efts secrete compounds that are repellent to most animals. The bright orange-and-red colour pattern of efts serves to warn of their noxious properties. If they sense danger, efts will adopt a defensive posture in which the tail is held high and curved above the back.

REPRODUCTION: Eggs are laid singly on submerged vegetation in spring. After about two months the larvae transform into efts, which then spend from one to three years on land, usually in woodlands. At the end of the eft stage, newts return to water. Adults are almost totally aquatic.

STATUS: COSEWIC: Not at risk.
OMNR: Not at risk.

AMBYSTOMATIDAE
Mole Salamanders

The 33 species of this family of salamanders occur only in North America. The Ambystomatidae includes several species that resemble one another very closely, making identification difficult. Identification is further confused by the presence of female "hybrids," which closely resemble their parental species, especially *Ambystoma jeffersonianum* and *A. laterale,* but also *A. texanum.*

The hybrids usually reproduce by gynogenesis, which means that although sperm from a male of a closely related species is required to initiate embryonic development, the offspring do not carry the male's genes and are genetically identical to their mother. Sometimes, however, especially at warmer temperatures, the male's genes are incorporated into the offspring, resulting in an increase in the number of chromosomes. The hybrids may have the usual diploid (2N) number of chromosomes, but they are most commonly triploid (3N). Sometimes tetraploid (4N) and even pentaploid (5N) individuals are found.

As their name implies, mole salamanders spend most of their time underground and are often unnoticed, even though they may be abundant in the area. Often they are seen only in spring, when they congregate at ponds to breed. The larvae resemble small adults, but have external gills. The larvae of all mole salamanders are similar in appearance, making them very difficult to identify. The adult colour patterns do not develop until the salamanders metamorphose and leave the breeding pond. Mole salamander larvae may be confused with larval lungless salamanders, but the latter do not breed in woodland ponds. Adult mole salamanders can be distinguished by the presence of a large parotoid gland above each shoulder behind the head.

BLUE-SPOTTED SALAMANDER
Ambystoma laterale
13 cm / 5"

Like most species of mole salamanders, Blue-spotted Salamanders are secretive and consequently are almost never seen except in spring, when they move to ponds to breed.

APPEARANCE: This is the smallest species of mole salamander, attaining a total length of up to 13 cm (5"). Adults are black above and grey below and are covered with small blue spots or flecks (upper and middle photos). Larvae have external gills and a large fin on the tail (lower photo).

▶ Adults closely resemble adult Jefferson and Small-mouthed salamanders, but these two species usually have fewer blue spots. Aquatic larvae are difficult to distinguish from those of other species of mole salamanders because the blue spots do not appear until the juvenile salamanders have left the pond (see Comparative Photographs, pp. 24–25; see also pp. 48–51).

HABITAT AND BEHAVIOUR: Adults inhabit most types of forest habitat, where they live in leaf litter on the forest floor or burrow in the soil. Activity is almost always nocturnal. Food consists of insects, earthworms, or other invertebrates. These salamanders are usually seen only in early spring, when they enter woodland ponds to breed. Breeding often occurs before the ice has completely disappeared from the ponds.

REPRODUCTION: Eggs are laid singly or in small clumps on submerged vegetation or on the bottom of the pond. The eggs hatch after a few weeks. Larvae transform in midsummer and leave the pond.

Blue-spotted Salamanders form hybrids with Jefferson Salamanders (pp. 48–49) and Small-mouthed Salamanders (pp. 50–51). These hybrids are all females and are difficult to distinguish from the parent species, although the hybrids are somewhat larger than the parent species.

STATUS: COSEWIC: Not at risk.
OMNR: Not at risk.

47

JEFFERSON SALAMANDER
Ambystoma jeffersonianum
20 cm / 8"

This species is named after Jefferson College in Washington County, Pennsylvania, where it was first collected. A close relative of the Blue-spotted Salamander, the Jefferson Salamander has less prominent blue markings.

APPEARANCE: Adults have a grey or brown back and lighter-coloured venter. Blue flecks may be present on the sides and limbs (upper and middle photos). Larvae are miniature versions of adults except that they have external gills and a large fin (lower photo). As with most salamander larvae, the forelimbs develop before the hindlimbs.

▶ Because the amount of blue flecking is variable, adults (especially females) may be confused with Blue-spotted and Small-mouthed salamanders. Identification of larvae can be difficult because adult colouring does not develop until the salamanders leave the breeding ponds (see Comparative Photographs, pp. 24–25; see also pp. 46–47, 50–51).

HABITAT AND BEHAVIOUR: Adults live on the forest floor, in the soil or in leaf litter. They are seldom seen except in early spring, when they move to woodland ponds to breed. Movement and breeding occur only at night, and most often on rainy nights.

REPRODUCTION: Eggs are laid in clumps attached to underwater vegetation. The eggs hatch after three or four weeks. At midsummer the larvae lose their gills and leave the pond. Jefferson Salamanders may breed with the closely related Blue-spotted Salamanders (pp. 46–47), producing hybrids. The hybrids are always female and often have triploid chromosome numbers, rather than the diploid number of the parent species. Hybrids, both larvae and adults, can be difficult to distinguish from the parent species.

STATUS: COSEWIC: Threatened. OMNR: Not at risk.

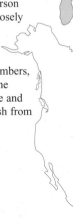

SMALL-MOUTHED SALAMANDER
Ambystoma texanum
14 cm / 6"

Although widespread in the central United States, Small-mouthed Salamanders have a very limited distribution in Canada.

APPEARANCE: Adults are black or very dark brown, with bluish or grey flecks on the sides (upper and middle photos). The amount of flecking can be quite variable. The head is proportionally smaller than the heads of other mole salamander species. Larvae resemble adults but are much smaller. They have external gills on the neck and a large fin on the tail (lower photo).

▶ Adult Small-mouthed Salamanders resemble Blue-spotted and Jefferson salamanders, although the two latter species usually have blue, rather than grey, flecks, configured in different patterns. Identification of larvae is difficult, because adult colouring does not develop until the juveniles leave the pond. In Ontario, Small-mouthed Salamanders occur only on Pelee Island, although hybrids of Small-mouthed and Blue-spotted salamanders have been found on the adjacent mainland (see Comparative Photographs, pp. 24–25; see also pp. 46–47, 48–49).

HABITAT AND BEHAVIOUR: Adults inhabit leaf litter on the forest floor and are usually seen only in spring, when they travel to ponds to breed. Movement and breeding take place almost exclusively at night.

REPRODUCTION: Eggs are attached to submerged branches or vegetation and hatch after a few weeks. The larvae have external gills, and the forelimbs develop before the hindlimbs. The larvae lose their gills and leave the pond in midsummer. Small-mouthed Salamanders may breed with Blue-spotted Salamanders (pp. 46–47) to produce hybrids. These hybrids are difficult to distinguish from their parent species, although hybrids are usually somewhat larger.

STATUS: COSEWIC: Vulnerable/ special concern. OMNR: Threatened.

SPOTTED SALAMANDER *Ambystoma maculatum*

20 cm / 8"

Although the colour pattern of this species makes identification easy, Spotted Salamanders are secretive and are not often seen outside the spring breeding season.

APPEARANCE: One of our largest salamanders, this species is easily recognized by the prominent yellow or orange spots on the back, tail, head, and legs. The background colour is black above and grey below (upper photo). The larvae superficially resemble adults, but are smaller, with proportionally larger heads, no spots, external gills, and a large tail fin (middle photo).

▶ The yellow spots make adults distinctive. Identification of juveniles can be difficult because the larvae of all species of mole salamanders are similar in appearance. The spots that characterize this species often do not appear until the juveniles have left the breeding ponds (see Comparative Photographs, pp. 24–25).

HABITAT AND BEHAVIOUR: Spotted Salamanders spend most of the year buried in the soil or leaf litter in woodlands, where they feed on worms, insects, and other invertebrates. The larvae are active predators, feeding on almost any available animal prey, including other salamander larvae. Spotted Salamanders are most often encountered in early spring, when they congregate at woodland ponds to breed. During this time, they are most active during periods of rain. All activity takes place at night.

REPRODUCTION: Eggs are laid in large clumps, in a jelly-like matrix, attached to submerged vegetation (lower photo). The egg masses resemble those of some frogs. The eggs hatch after about four weeks. The larval stage is short; the young lose their gills and leave the pond in midsummer.

STATUS: COSEWIC: Not at risk. OMNR: Not at risk.

PLETHODONTIDAE
Lungless Salamanders

This family contains over 200 species, more than any other family of salamanders, and includes some of the most common and widespread Ontario species. Salamanders of this family have no lungs as adults but obtain oxygen through their skin, especially the lining of the mouth. Some lungless salamander species deposit their eggs in water, but others deposit eggs on land, in protected spots such as rotten logs. They are not completely independent of water, however, because the eggs must be in a moist environment to prevent them from drying out.

Members of this family may be confused with mole salamanders, although lungless salamanders are usually more slender, have shorter legs, and attain a smaller maximum size. A groove runs from each nostril downward to the upper lip; this groove may be visible only under magnification. The larvae of lungless salamanders may resemble the larvae of mole salamanders but can usually be distinguished from them by the habitat in which they are found. Mole salamander larvae are usually found in woodland ponds, while lungless salamanders prefer streams, seepage areas, or sphagnum bogs.

NORTHERN DUSKY SALAMANDER
Desmognathus fuscus
15 cm / 6"

Northern Dusky Salamanders are abundant in eastern North America, including Quebec and New Brunswick, although they are relatively rare in Ontario.

APPEARANCE: Adults are brown with an irregular darker line along each side of the back (upper photo). Dark flecks may also be present on the back and sides. The underside is lighter in colour. There is a distinctive light stripe from the eye to the angle of the jaw (middle photo). The tail usually has a ridge along its top rather than being round in cross-section. Total length can be up to about 15 cm (6"), but most individuals are smaller. The larvae resemble adults except that they have yellowish bellies and external gills on the neck (lower photo).

▶ Northern Dusky Salamanders are more heavy-bodied than most lungless salamanders, and the hindlegs are longer and sturdier than the forelegs. The light stripe on the side of the head is also diagnostic (see Comparative Photographs, pp. 24–25).

HABITAT AND BEHAVIOUR: This species prefers small streams or wet seepage areas and can usually be found under stones or in thick vegetation, either in water or at the water's edge. Food consists of aquatic insects or other invertebrates.

Northern Dusky Salamanders were once thought to be absent from Ontario, but they have been found in the Niagara region. It is not known whether they have been present and undetected for many years or whether they have recently crossed the Niagara River from the United States.

REPRODUCTION: Eggs are deposited in clumps among vegetation or under stones, in or near water. The eggs hatch in early summer, and the larvae spend about two months in the water before transforming.

STATUS: COSEWIC: Not at risk. OMNR: Not at risk.

NORTHERN TWO-LINED SALAMANDER
Eurycea bislineata
12 cm / 5"

Northern Two-lined Salamanders are typically found in streams, where their slender shape affords them increased agility. During the summer they may leave water and move into adjacent woodlands.

APPEARANCE: Adults are yellow on the back and belly, with two broad dark lines down the back. The sides may be darkly mottled (upper and middle photos). The belly is usually a paler shade of yellow than the back. The larvae resemble adults but are smaller, with small external gills and a fin on the tail (lower photo).

▶ Northern Dusky, Eastern-Red-backed, and Four-toed salamanders are more heavy-bodied than Northern Two-lined Salamanders. Northern Dusky Salamanders are found in streams; Eastern Red-backed and Four-toed salamanders may also be found in forest-floor habitat (see Comparative Photographs, pp. 24–25).

HABITAT AND BEHAVIOUR: The slender body shape, with short limbs, is an adaptation to life in fast-moving water. Adults usually inhabit streams in wooded areas. They often leave the stream to forage in the leaf litter on the forest floor during the summer, returning to the stream in the fall. During the summer they can travel up to several hundred metres from the stream. Movement is related to rainfall; dry periods are spent buried in leaf litter or the soil, while a rainy night will initiate movement. Food consists of insects, worms, and other invertebrates. Winter is spent in sheltered locations in streams or buried in the stream bed.

REPRODUCTION: Eggs are laid under stones or other objects in the stream bed. Larvae may metamorphose after a few months or may not transform until the following summer. The newly transformed young salamanders leave the stream to forage on land, returning to water in the fall.

STATUS: COSEWIC: Not at risk.
OMNR: Not at risk.

FOUR-TOED SALAMANDER
Hemidactylium scutatum

10 cm / 4"

Four-toed Salamanders are often found in sphagnum bogs, unlike most other Ontario salamander species.

APPEARANCE: This species can be easily identified by the four toes on the hindfoot. Adult Four-toed Salamanders have a reddish- or grey-brown back (upper photo) and a distinctive white belly with black spots (middle photo). There is a constriction at the base of the tail. If the tail is bitten by a predator, it will break away, while the salamander escapes. Larvae have external gills and resemble the adults somewhat, although the adult colour pattern may not appear until after metamorphosis (lower photo).

▶ All other Ontario salamander species except the Mudpuppy have five toes on the hindfoot. The belly colour pattern and basal tail constriction will distinguish Four-toed Salamanders from other forest-floor species (see Comparative Photographs, pp. 24–25).

HABITAT AND BEHAVIOUR: Typical habitat of adults is sphagnum bogs, although they are also found in moist woodland. Habitat use is moisture-dependent; salamanders will forage in forested areas if there is sufficient rainfall or ground moisture but will retreat to wet bogs during dry periods. Newly transformed juveniles may remain in their bog habitat or move into nearby woodland. Four-toed Salamanders feed on insects, worms, and other invertebrates. Winter is spent buried in the soil in wooded areas.

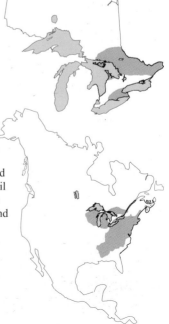

REPRODUCTION: Mating occurs in autumn, but the eggs are not laid until the following spring. Eggs are deposited in sphagnum at or near the edges of open pools in bogs. Several females may deposit eggs in the same location, and the females remain with the eggs until they hatch. After hatching, the larvae crawl down through the sphagnum and into the water. In late summer, the larvae transform and leave the water.

STATUS: COSEWIC: Not at risk.
OMNR: Not at risk.

EASTERN RED-BACKED SALAMANDER
Plethodon cinereus
10 cm / 4"

Eastern Red-backed Salamanders are a common species, and in many areas of suitable habitat they may be the most abundant vertebrate. Because of their secretive habits, however, they are rarely seen.

APPEARANCE: Adult Eastern Red-backed Salamanders can measure up to 10 cm (4"), although most are smaller. The sides are black or dark grey and the venter is mottled grey and white. Dorsal colour is variable, and two main colour forms are found. The typical colour is red, sometimes shading to orange, brown, or yellow (upper and middle photos). The second colour form (called the lead-backed colour phase) has a grey back (lower photo). The proportions of red-backed and lead-backed forms can vary greatly in local populations. Some red-backed individuals have a series of black dots or even a thin black line down the centre of the back, creating two red stripes.

▶ The variable colouring of Eastern Red-backed Salamanders can lead to confusion with other forest-floor species. Four-toed Salamanders have a white belly and basal tail constriction. Northern Dusky Salamanders are heavy-bodied. Northern Two-lined Salamanders are very slender (see Comparative Photographs, pp. 24–25).

HABITAT AND BEHAVIOUR: Eastern Red-backed Salamanders feed on worms, insects, and other forest-floor invertebrates. They prefer moist soil in forested areas, where they burrow in the leaf litter or the soil. They may move about on rainy nights, but they typically travel shorter distances than other salamander species. They overwinter in soil.

REPRODUCTION: Eastern Red-backed Salamanders have a distinctive mode of reproduction whereby they do not enter water at any stage of their reproductive cycle. The eggs are laid on land and the entire larval stage occurs inside the egg. Eggs are laid in moist spots, usually under or in rotting logs. The eggs are in a clump, usually attached to the "ceiling" of a small cavity in or under the log. Females may remain with their eggs until they hatch. The young salamanders resemble adults.

STATUS: COSEWIC: Not at risk. OMNR: Not at risk.

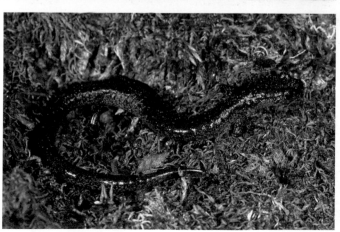

FROGS AND TOADS

BUFONIDAE
Toads

This family contains almost 300 species worldwide, with two species occurring in Ontario. Toads have thick warty skin and bony head crests, with a familiar stocky, short-legged body shape. Toads move by walking, rather than jumping like most other frogs. They have large glands, called parotoid glands, one above each shoulder, behind the head. These glands, along with the smaller warts, produce secretions that are repellent and sometimes toxic to potential predators. Toad skin is thicker than that of most other frogs and offers some protection against water loss. Eggs are laid in strings in shallow water. Tadpoles are small and black, and they usually congregate in schools. Toads transform at a small size. Although they can extend their tongues to catch prey, toads feed mostly on terrestrial insects and worms, rather than on flying insects.

AMERICAN TOAD *Bufo americanus*

11 cm / 4"

Probably our most familiar amphibian, American Toads can be found near homes or in gardens and may occur in surprisingly large numbers in a favourable habitat.

APPEARANCE: The dorsal colour is usually brown with black, reddish, or darker brown markings. The dark dorsal blotches usually contain one or two warts (upper photo). There may be a narrow white stripe down the middle of the back. More colourful individuals occur towards the northern part of the range. The venter is white with dark spots or mottling. Tadpoles are small and black; they usually congregate in shallow water, often in large numbers (middle photo).

▶ Fowler's Toads are found in Ontario only on the northern shores of Lake Erie; their dark dorsal blotches contain three or more warts (see Comparative Photographs, pp. 26–27).

HABITAT AND BEHAVIOUR: The thick skin of American Toads reduces water loss and allows them to inhabit locations drier than those available to many other amphibian species. They can often be found near human habitation, and individuals may remain in a garden or other favourable location all summer. They feed on insects, slugs, and worms. Toads overwinter by burrowing into the soil and may dig down to depths of more than a metre.

REPRODUCTION: American Toads congregate in the spring to breed. The males emit a prolonged trilling call (lower photo), and a loud chorus can be produced by males calling from a breeding pond. The females gravitate toward the sound. Toads are "explosive breeders," meaning that they arrive at the pond more or less simultaneously and within a few days they all mate, deposit their eggs, and depart. Eggs are laid in long strands on the bottom of the pond or among vegetation. Newly hatched tadpoles are very small, but they grow quickly and transform after about two months. Because most eggs are laid within a short period of time, transformation occurs more or less simultaneously. Many tiny toads leave the pond together and disperse into the surrounding area.

STATUS: COSEWIC: Not at risk. OMNR: Not at risk.

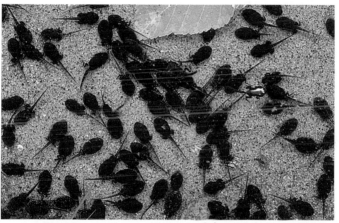

FOWLER'S TOAD *Bufo fowleri*

10 cm / 4"

Fowler's Toad is rare in Ontario and justifiably listed as threatened. Even within its small range, it is found only in some sandy habitats near the Lake Erie shore.

APPEARANCE: The background colour is brown, sometimes shading to grey, with irregular darker markings. The dark dorsal blotches contain three or more warts (upper and middle photos). The belly is usually unspotted, although some individuals have a single central spot. Tadpoles have the typical toad-like form, small and dark (lower photo), and are often found in large numbers.

▶ This species resembles the American Toad, and distinguishing between the two may be difficult. In American Toads the dark dorsal blotches contain only one or two warts and the belly is extensively mottled. Tadpoles of the two species are very similar. Fowler's Toads are found only near the shore of Lake Erie, while American Toads are widespread in Ontario (see Comparative Photographs, pp. 26–27; see also pp. 66–67).

HABITAT AND BEHAVIOUR: Outside the breeding season, Fowler's Toads are found only in terrestrial habitats. Adults spend the summer in a variety of habitats and can be found in meadows, cultivated land, or woods. They feed on worms and ground-dwelling insects. When the tadpoles transform in midsummer, they leave the water and spend the remainder of the summer on land. With the onset of cold weather, they burrow into the soil to overwinter.

REPRODUCTION: Fowler's Toads breed in early spring, late March or April, and many individuals may breed in the same pond. Males produce a trill that lasts only two to three seconds, much shorter than the trill of the American Toad. The two species have been known to hybridize in locations where both occur.

STATUS: COSEWIC: Threatened. OMNR: Threatened.

HYLIDAE
Treefrogs

This family contains about 400 species worldwide, varying
in size from tiny to very large. Not all treefrogs live in trees.
Of the five Ontario species belonging to the Hylidae, only
two are normally found in trees or shrubs. Treefrogs can
usually be distinguished by small or large discs on the tips
of their toes, which allow the frogs to climb; climbing
species usually have larger discs than ground dwellers.
Tropical treefrogs may deposit their eggs in unusual
locations, even in small amounts of water captured in
flowers or leaf rosettes, sometimes high in trees, and some
species carry their eggs on their back until they hatch. All
Ontario treefrogs, however, deposit their eggs in water and
have a swimming tadpole stage.

GRAY TREEFROG *Hyla versicolor*

6 cm / 2.5"

Gray Treefrogs are not often seen because of their colour pattern and secretive habits. They are best seen on rainy nights in spring or fall.

APPEARANCE: This species is Ontario's largest treefrog. Dorsal colour pattern is usually a mottled grey or brown (upper photo), although individual frogs can change colour from brown to green. A white patch is always present below the eye. Juveniles are bright green (middle photo). Patches of yellow or orange on the thighs are visible only when the legs are extended. The venter is white. Males have a dark-coloured throat, while in females and juveniles the throat is white. The skin is rough with small warts. Large discs are present at the tips of the toes. Tadpoles can be up to 5 cm (2") long and have distinctive reddish colouring on the fin (lower photo).

▶ Adults are larger than adults of any other Ontario treefrog species, and the green colour of juveniles is distinctive. Although toads have rough warty skin, they are generally brown in colour and lack toe discs. *Hyla versicolor* is a tetraploid (4N) species, with twice the normal number of chromosomes. It is closely related to the similar-appearing diploid (2N) species *Hyla chrysoscelis,* which is found in Manitoba and the central United States.

HABITAT AND BEHAVIOUR: Gray Treefrogs spend much of their time in trees or shrubs, feeding on insects, but they sometimes travel on the ground on rainy nights. Juveniles and adults can climb surprisingly high in trees. They are not easily seen against a background of bark or lichen but when they jump the bright "flash colour" on the legs is startling. They are not often seen outside the breeding season. Gray Treefrogs spend the winter in leaf litter or buried in the soil.

REPRODUCTION: In late spring, Gray Treefrogs congregate in woodland ponds to breed. The males emit their slow trill from trees, shrubs, or other vegetation above the water. Eggs are deposited in floating bunches, each consisting of several dozen eggs, and hatch within a week. The tadpole stage lasts about two months, with the young transforming in late summer.

STATUS: COSEWIC: Not at risk.
OMNR: Not at risk.

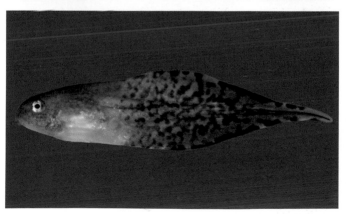

NORTHERN CRICKET FROG *Acris crepitans*

2.5 cm / 1"

The Northern Cricket Frog is one of Ontario's rarest vertebrate species. Its small size and colour make it difficult to see in its preferred water's-edge habitat.

APPEARANCE: This small treefrog is usually brown or greenish-grey with faint dorsal markings, a triangular mark between the eyes, and crossbands on the top of the thighs (upper and middle photos). The belly is white, and the throat may be yellow in males. The skin is warty and the toe discs are small. There is a dark line along the rear surface of the thigh. Tadpoles are up to 3.5 cm (1.4") long, with dark flecks and a black tail tip (lower photo).

► Western Chorus Frogs are similar in size to Northern Cricket Frogs but have stripes along the back and are much more widespread in Ontario than Northern Cricket Frogs (see Comparative Photographs, pp. 26–27).

HABITAT AND BEHAVIOUR: Northern Cricket Frogs are terrestrial and are usually found at the margins of permanent ponds, in both woodlands and meadows. They do not climb into trees or bushes. Food is small insects and other terrestrial invertebrates. Northern Cricket Frogs overwinter at or near the surface of the soil, in leaf litter. In Ontario, they are found only on Pelee Island in Lake Erie, and they have not been found there in recent years. Because of their limited distribution, they are considered endangered in Canada, although they are widespread and abundant in the United States.

REPRODUCTION: Mating occurs in late spring. The call of male Northern Cricket Frogs resembles the sound of stones rapidly clicked together. Eggs are laid singly on the bottom of ponds or attached to underwater vegetation. The eggs hatch quickly, but the tadpole stage is longer than in many other treefrog species; transformation occurs in August or even September. Afterwards, juveniles leave the water and join the adults in terrestrial habitats.

STATUS: COSEWIC: Endangered.
OMNR: Endangered.

75

SPRING PEEPER *Pseudacris crucifer*

3.5 cm / 1.5"

One of our best-known harbingers of spring, the call of the Spring Peeper signals the arrival of warm weather.

APPEARANCE: Dorsal colour ranges from light to dark brown (upper photo), sometimes with a reddish or grey wash. A darker, roughly X-shaped mark is always present on the back (middle photo). Yellow may be present at the base of the hindlegs, visible only when the leg is extended. The underside is whitish with occasional dark flecks. The skin is smooth and the toes have small discs at their extremities. Tadpoles are up to 3 cm (1.25") in total length. Dorsal colour is greenish with gold flecks; ventral colour is iridescent white. The fins are transparent, often with dark blotches at the edges (lower photo).

▶ Northern Cricket, Western Chorus, and Boreal Chorus frogs are the same size but lack the X-shaped mark on the back and seldom climb above ground level (see Comparative Photographs, pp. 26–27).

HABITAT AND BEHAVIOUR: Following the breeding season, adult Spring Peepers spend the summer in leaf litter in wooded areas. Although Spring Peepers can climb, they are seldom found more than a metre above ground. Spring Peepers overwinter in leaf litter. Their body chemistry allows them to withstand temperatures a few degrees below freezing.

REPRODUCTION: In spring, these treefrogs congregate at breeding ponds, even before the ponds are completely ice-free. Suitable sites are typically shallow, often temporary ponds in woodlands, although ponds in unforested areas and the shallow margins of larger water bodies are also used. The Spring Peeper is one of the first frogs to breed in spring, often as early as March in southern Ontario. Males occupy small territories in the ponds and emit their distinctive ear-piercing *peep* from floating branches, pond edges, or low vegetation above water. Eggs are laid singly or in small clumps, attached to underwater vegetation. The eggs hatch after two to three weeks; the tadpoles transform after about three months.

STATUS: COSEWIC: Not at risk. OMNR: Not at risk.

WESTERN CHORUS FROG *Pseudacris triseriata*

3 cm / 1"

Western Chorus Frogs are one of the first frog species to begin breeding in the spring. The short larval period allows this species to breed in shallow temporary water bodies.

APPEARANCE: The background dorsal colour is brown. A darker stripe runs through the eye and down the side of the body, and there are three other variable dark stripes on the back (upper and middle photos). There is usually a dark marking on the top of the head between the eyes. The underside is off-white and the belly skin has a granular texture. The body shape is more elongate than that of other treefrogs. The toes are long and the toe discs are very small. The tadpoles are small and have transparent fins covered with small dark flecks (lower photo).

▶ The Boreal Chorus Frog has similar markings and shorter hindlimbs. In Ontario, the two species have widely separated distributions: the Western Chorus Frog occurs in the southern part of the province; the Boreal Chorus Frog occurs in the north and northwest (see Comparative Photographs, pp. 26–27; see also pp. 80–81).

HABITAT AND BEHAVIOUR: Western Chorus Frogs can be found in woodlands, meadows, and cultivated land. They are not good climbers but occasionally climb into low vegetation. Adults are difficult to find and are seldom seen outside the breeding season. Food consists of small insects, spiders, and slugs. The winter is spent in leaf litter or shallow soil. Western Chorus Frogs can withstand temperatures a few degrees below freezing.

REPRODUCTION: Western Chorus Frogs emerge in early spring and may begin calling before the breeding ponds are completely ice-free. They breed in open ponds or ditches, sometimes even in urban areas. Males call from the water's edge or from emergent vegetation a few centimetres above ground or water level. The call is similar to the sound produced by running a fingernail along the teeth of a comb. Eggs are laid in small clumps and attached to submerged vegetation. The eggs hatch after about two weeks. The larval period is fairly short, and the young frogs leave the water in midsummer.

STATUS: COSEWIC: Not at risk. OMNR: Not at risk.

BOREAL CHORUS FROG *Pseudacris maculata*

3 cm / 1"

Although the distinctive call of Boreal Chorus Frogs informs us of their presence, they are difficult to see because their colour pattern blends into the background vegetation.

APPEARANCE: The background colour is grey or brown, sometimes green, with a dark stripe through the eye and down the side of the body. The back has three other dark stripes (upper and middle photos), although these may be broken up into dashes or spots (lower photo). There may be a dark marking on the top of the head between the eyes. The belly skin has a granular texture and is white in colour. The body of chorus frogs is more elongate than that of other treefrogs. Tadpoles are small, with small dark flecks on the tail fins, very similar in appearance to Western Chorus Frog tadpoles.

▶ The Boreal Chorus Frog resembles the Western Chorus Frog. Until 1989 they were considered to be the same species. They have similar markings, but the Western Chorus Frog has relatively longer hindlimbs. Boreal Chorus Frogs move in short hops rather than long leaps like other chorus frogs. In Ontario, the Boreal Chorus Frog occurs in the north and northwest; the Western Chorus Frog occurs in the south; their Ontario ranges do not overlap (see Comparative Photographs, pp. 26–27; see also pp. 78–79).

HABITAT AND BEHAVIOUR: Boreal Chorus Frogs are usually found in woodlands and meadows and may climb into low vegetation. Adults are seldom seen outside the breeding season. Food consists of small insects and other invertebrates. They spend the winter buried in the soil.

REPRODUCTION: Boreal Chorus Frogs emerge in very early spring, often calling before the ice has left the breeding areas. They breed in ponds or ditches, usually in treeless spots but sometimes in wooded areas. Males call from the water's edge or in vegetation above the water. The call is like the sound produced by a fingernail on the teeth of a comb. Eggs are attached to submerged vegetation, in small clumps. The eggs hatch after about two weeks, and the larval period is fairly short. The young frogs leave the water in midsummer and disperse into the surrounding area.

STATUS: COSEWIC: Not at risk. OMNR: Not at risk.

RANIDAE
True Frogs

The Ranidae is the largest amphibian family. It is found on
most continents and contains about 600 species worldwide.
These frogs are most abundant in Asia and Africa, with only
six species occurring in Ontario. When one thinks of a typical
frog, it is the body shape, good jumping ability, aquatic
tadpoles, and distinctive mating calls of this family that come
to mind. True Frogs are usually found near water, whether
small streams, large lakes, rapids, or stagnant ponds. Eggs
are usually deposited in water, and the tadpoles have a variety
of adaptations to their particular habitat, especially in the
tropics. In Ontario, some members of this family spend one
or more winters as tadpoles before transforming into adults.

WOOD FROG *Rana sylvatica*

6.5 cm / 2.5"

The Wood Frog is the most widespread frog species in Canada and occurs farther north than any other North American amphibian species.

APPEARANCE: Compared to other members of the Ranidae, the Wood Frog is a small species. The back is usually brown, although many individuals have a reddish or copper tinge (upper photo). There is a distinctive dark brown bar behind the eye and a thin dark line from the nostril to the eye. These dark marks provide a strong contrast with the white upper lip. There are two folds of skin along the back, and these are often darker or lighter than the background colour. Below these folds the sides are usually darkly mottled. The hindlegs often have dark crossbands (middle photo). The underside is white, sometimes with darker mottling. Some northern Wood Frogs have a light line down the middle of the back, but this is rare in southern populations. Tadpoles are 3–4 cm (1–1.5") long and darkly flecked; the coiled intestine can be seen through the transparent belly skin (lower photo).

▶ No other Ontario frog has the combination of small size, brownish unpatterned back, and dark head markings (see Comparative Photographs, pp. 26–27).

HABITAT AND BEHAVIOUR: Wood Frogs prefer forest-floor habitat but may travel across open areas on rainy nights. They feed on insects and are great consumers of mosquitoes. Wood Frogs burrow into the soil to overwinter. They can tolerate below-freezing temperatures.

REPRODUCTION: Wood Frogs congregate at ponds to breed in spring. They prefer ponds in woodlands and may even use temporary ponds. The males produce a quacking call. Eggs are laid in a clump attached to vegetation below the surface of the water. Several females may deposit their eggs in the same location. The breeding season is short; after breeding, Wood Frogs spend the spring and summer on the forest floor. The larval period lasts about two months, allowing the young frogs to transform before the breeding ponds dry up. Juvenile frogs often travel long distances through the forest.

STATUS: COSEWIC: Not at risk.
OMNR: Not at risk.

NORTHERN LEOPARD FROG *Rana pipiens*

11 cm / 4"

The Northern Leopard Frog is probably our most familiar frog species. They are highly mobile and may travel considerable distances overland. Northern Leopard Frogs have a wide distribution in Ontario and are found in a variety of habitats.

APPEARANCE: The dorsal colour is usually green, occasionally brown, with dark spots outlined in white (upper and middle photos). There is a prominent light-coloured fold down each side of the back. The belly is white, and there may be a yellow wash on the throat and lips. Males and females are similar in appearance. Tadpoles have pointed tails and are mottled (lower photo); some have a bluish wash. In some tadpoles the belly skin may be transparent, allowing the coiled intestine to be seen.

▶ Northern Leopard Frogs resemble Pickerel Frogs, and the two species can be confused. The tadpoles are especially difficult to distinguish, but the adults are easier to tell apart. In Northern Leopard Frogs the dark spots on the back are usually round or oval and randomly arranged; in Pickerel Frogs they are squarish in shape and usually arranged in two rows along the back (see Comparative Photographs, pp. 26–27; see also pp. 88–89).

HABITAT AND BEHAVIOUR: Adults spend the summer in open fields or meadows, where they feed chiefly on insects. Tadpoles feed on algae and other small food particles. Newly transformed juveniles often travel overland in search of new habitats. Winter is usually spent at the bottom of a body of water.

REPRODUCTION: Northern Leopard Frogs breed in early spring in ponds or larger bodies of water. The call is a prolonged drone or snore-like sound. Eggs are deposited in clumps and are attached to submerged vegetation or other objects. A number of females may lay their eggs in the same location, so a suitable site could have many such clumps, each with 4000–6000 eggs. Tadpoles transform in late summer.

STATUS: COSEWIC: Not at risk. OMNR: Not at risk.

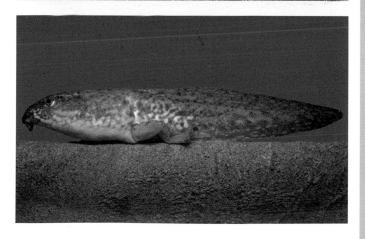

PICKEREL FROG *Rana palustris*

9 cm / 3.5"

Although superficially similar to the Northern Leopard Frog, the Pickerel Frog is smaller, less widely distributed, and more likely to be found in wooded areas.

APPEARANCE: The dorsal background colour is brown, sometimes golden or cream, but never green, with a prominent bronze fold down each side of the back. The dorsal dark spots are squarish and typically aligned in two longitudinal rows (upper and middle photos). The venter is white, often with some yellow or orange at the base of the hindlegs. Males and females are similar in appearance. Tadpoles resemble those of the Northern Leopard Frog; they are flecked or mottled and have pointed tails (lower photo).

▶ Pickerel Frogs are similar to Northern Leopard Frogs in size and appearance, but in Northern Leopard Frogs the dark spots are round or oval, not square, and the background colour is usually green rather than brown. It can be difficult to distinguish between tadpoles of these two species (see Comparative Photographs, pp. 26–27; see also pp. 86–87).

HABITAT AND BEHAVIOUR: Adults spend the summer away from open water, in meadows or woodlands, although they usually remain near damp locations. Following metamorphosis, juvenile frogs travel overland, often considerable distances from their place of birth. Pickerel Frogs overwinter at the bottom of ponds or other bodies of water. The skin secretions of the Pickerel Frog are repellent to some predators and may be toxic to other frogs.

REPRODUCTION: Pickerel Frogs breed in ponds, streams, or springs. Males produce a low-pitched snoring call and may even call underwater. Eggs are laid in clumps and attached to submerged vegetation. The tadpoles spend a few months growing, then transform in late summer or early fall.

STATUS: COSEWIC: Not at risk. OMNR: Not at risk.

GREEN FROG *Rana clamitans*

10 cm / 4"

Green Frogs may be confused with other large frog species found in similar aquatic habitats.

APPEARANCE: Dorsal colour can be variable but is typically green, with darker spots that may be numerous or absent, and with crossbands on the thighs (upper photo). Some individuals are brownish. The belly and throat are white, sometimes with a yellowish wash. In males the throat is distinctly yellow and the eardrum is larger than the eye (middle photo); in females the eardrum is approximately the same diameter as the eye (upper photo). Tadpoles measure up to 8 cm (3") long; they are mottled above with a white opaque belly and a rounded tail tip.

▶ Mink Frogs have irregular blotches on the thighs rather than narrow crossbands. American Bullfrogs do not have folds along each side of the back. Green Frog tadpoles resemble Mink Frog tadpoles, and the two are difficult to distinguish. Newly transformed juvenile frogs (lower photo) may also be difficult to identify (see Comparative Photographs, pp. 26–27; see also pp. 92–93, 94–95).

HABITAT AND BEHAVIOUR: Green Frogs are typically found in or near permanent water. When approached while on land, Green Frogs sit motionless and wait until the last minute before jumping to safety into water. They dive immediately, unlike Mink Frogs or American Bullfrogs, which "skip" across the water surface before diving. During the extended breeding season, males set up territories and may fight to defend them. Newly transformed juveniles disperse overland in search of new habitat. During this dispersal period, young Green Frogs can be found in a variety of terrestrial locations. Adults, however, are seldom found far from water. Adult Green Frogs overwinter underwater.

REPRODUCTION: Breeding begins in early summer and may continue until August. The call of the male is a single twanging note. Eggs are deposited in a single layer at the water surface. Tadpoles often congregate in deeper water, away from the shore, sheltering under lily pads. Tadpoles overwinter and transform the summer after the eggs are laid.

STATUS: COSEWIC: Not at risk. OMNR: Not at risk.

MINK FROG *Rana septentrionalis*

7.5 cm / 3"

Mink Frogs occur farther north than many other large frog species. The name comes from the characteristic mink-like odour emitted by the adults when they are handled.

APPEARANCE: The dorsal colour pattern of the Mink Frog is a green background with variable dark mottling. There is a fold on each side of the back, prominent toward the head and becoming less visible toward the posterior. The hindlegs have irregular dark blotches (upper photo). Mink Frogs are usually more darkly mottled than Green Frogs or American Bullfrogs, but this is not a reliable character for distinguishing these species. The throat is often tinged with yellow, and in males this yellow colour can be very prominent. In females, the eardrum is approximately the same size as the eye (upper photo), while in males the eardrum is larger than the eye (middle photo). Tadpoles grow up to 8 cm (3") long and have a pinkish wash, dorsal mottling, and an opaque white belly (lower photo).

▶ American Bullfrogs have no folds on the back. In Green Frogs the hindlegs are crossbanded, whereas in Mink Frogs they are blotched. Tadpoles of Mink Frogs are difficult to distinguish from Green Frog tadpoles (see Comparative Photographs, pp. 26–27).

HABITAT AND BEHAVIOUR: Mink Frogs occupy permanent water and prefer ponds or lakes with lily pads. Newly transformed juveniles travel overland in search of new aquatic habitat. Once established in suitable habitat, adults seldom venture far from water, spending the winter at the bottom of their home pond. When they feel threatened, Mink Frogs escape by entering the water. They usually "skip" across the surface before diving, while Green Frogs dive immediately.

REPRODUCTION: Mink Frogs breed from early summer to mid-August in permanent water. Males produce a repetitive knocking call. Eggs are attached to submerged vegetation and hatch after a few days. This species spends one winter as a tadpole before transforming.

STATUS: COSEWIC: Not at risk.
OMNR: Not at risk.

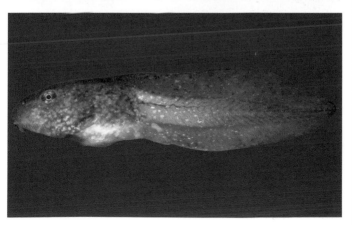

93

AMERICAN BULLFROG *Rana catesbeiana*

15 cm / 6"

Ontario's largest frog species is found only in larger bodies of permanent water, where its calls are a familiar sound of summer.

APPEARANCE: The back is medium green, with a pattern varying from only a few small dark spots (upper photo) to extensive dark mottling. The underside is white with occasional mottling. The throat is often tinged with yellow and may be bright yellow in males (middle photo). In males the eardrum is larger than the eye; in females it is about the same diameter as the eye. Tadpoles grow up to 10 cm (4") in length, have a white opaque belly, and are covered with small black dots (lower photo).

▶ Mottled American Bullfrogs may be confused with Green Frogs or Mink Frogs, but American Bullfrogs have no folds along the sides of the back. These folds are present in the other two species. Tadpoles of Green and Mink frogs are usually mottled with dark blotches rather than small dots (see Comparative Photographs, pp. 26–27).

HABITAT AND BEHAVIOUR: Adults seldom move far from permanent water, but young frogs travel in search of new habitat, often overland. Winter is spent underwater. When bullfrogs escape to water after being alarmed, they often "skip" across the surface before diving, while Green Frogs dive without skipping. American Bullfrogs consume insects, other aquatic invertebrates, and other frogs.

REPRODUCTION: American Bullfrogs usually breed in June, later than most other amphibian species. The breeding period is extended over several weeks. Unlike those species that breed in early spring in shallow or temporary pools, bullfrogs prefer deeper, permanent water. Males set up territories in suitable breeding areas and advertise by emitting a distinctive two- or three-note bass call. Females are attracted by the calls and choose a mate on the basis of his territory. Females can produce up to 8000 eggs, which form a floating mat at the water surface. The eggs hatch after a few days, and the larvae spend one or two winters as tadpoles before transforming.

STATUS: COSEWIC: Not at risk.
OMNR: Not at risk.

AMPHIBIANS THAT MAY OCCUR IN ONTARIO

TIGER SALAMANDER *Ambystoma tigrinum*
25 cm / 10"

One of the largest mole salamanders, the Tiger Salamander is black with olive blotches. Tiger Salamanders are widely distributed in western Canada and the United States. In Ontario they were known from Point Pelee and Pelee Island but have not been found there recently. This species has been designated as extirpated from Ontario by both COSEWIC and OMNR.

SPRING SALAMANDER *Gyrinophilus porphyriticus*
20 cm / 8"

One of the largest members of the family Plethodontidae, this species ranges from pink to light brown in colour, with darker mottling. There is usually a light line from the eye to the nostril. Spring Salamanders are found in streams and are usually the largest salamander in a stream community. This species was reported from the Niagara River area in 1877 but has never been seen again in Ontario. It is found south of the Great Lakes and the St. Lawrence River in Quebec and the United States.

RED SALAMANDER *Pseudotriton ruber*
18 cm / 7"

This heavy-bodied, short-legged salamander is red or reddish-brown with black spots. It is found primarily in streams or wet seepage areas, although individuals may travel away from water. A few Red Salamanders were reported from the Parry Sound District in 1946 but the species has never been seen again in Ontario. It is likely that these salamanders were brought in by anglers from the United States to be used as bait and later released. The Red Salamander is widespread in the eastern United States.

SPECIES ACCOUNTS
REPTILES OF ONTARIO

Reptiles in Ontario are represented by eight species of turtle, one lizard, and 15 snake species. Reptiles differ from amphibians in having waterproof scaly skin, toes (where present) with claws, and no gills at any stage in their life cycle.

Turtles

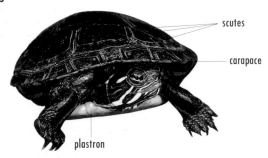

Turtles are unique among living vertebrates because of their shell. The structure of the shell is formed by the ribs, broadened and fused together. The vertebral column is fused to the carapace, the upper portion of the shell. The shell's outer covering consists of enlarged scales called scutes.

The shell provides protection. The limbs, head, and tail can be pulled directly into the shell or tucked under its edge. In Snapping Turtles, Stinkpots, and Softshells, the lower part of the shell, or plastron, is reduced in size. This limits the amount of protection that the shell offers but allows more leg movement. Except for Snapping Turtles, female turtles are usually larger than males.

Some limitations are imposed by the shell. Its size and weight reduces the turtle's mobility. In female turtles, the number of eggs that can be produced is limited by the space available inside the shell.

Ontario's eight species of turtles are members of four families. Three of these families are represented in Ontario by only one species. The remaining five species are in the family Emydidae.

Lizards

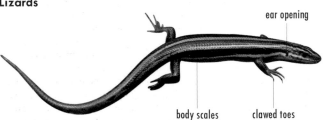

Lizards are abundant and diverse in tropical areas but rare in more temperate zones. Most lizards are carnivorous and feed on insects, worms, frogs, rodents, or other prey, depending on the lizard's size. A few lizards are herbivorous.

Almost all lizards lay eggs, although a few species bear live young. The eggs are deposited in leaf litter, rotting logs, or under stones. In general, lizards, unlike turtles, do not dig nest holes for their eggs.

Lizards bear a superficial resemblance to salamanders, although the differences are obvious on closer examination. Like most reptiles, lizards have dry scaly skin, external ear openings, and claws on their toes, while salamanders have smooth, moist, scaleless skin, no ear openings, and no claws. Lizards are fast-moving and usually prefer drier habitat, while salamanders are much less agile and are almost always found in moist habitats.

Only five lizard species occur in Canada, one in Ontario. The latter is a member of the skink family, a diverse family with a worldwide distribution. Typical skinks have smooth scales and strong limbs, but in some species the limbs are reduced or even absent, and the scales may be enlarged and roughened.

Snakes

upper lip

lower lip

scale rows

belly scales

Snakes have adapted to many habitats and can be found in tall trees, the open ocean, deserts, fresh water, and underground.

Most snake species reproduce by laying eggs, but many species are live-bearing. Egg-layers deposit their eggs in sheltered spots under stones and logs or in leaf litter. Incubation time depends on the temperature of the nest. In some species the female guards the eggs and may coil around them to protect and even warm them slightly.

Snakes do not smell by inhaling air. Instead, they pick up scents on the tongue, which they then insert into a pocket on the roof of the mouth, where the scents are interpreted. This is why snakes flick their tongues.

Snakes have no external ears, so they cannot hear airborne sounds. They are, however, very sensitive to vibrations in the ground, alerting them of potential danger.

99

TURTLES

CHELYDRIDAE
Snapping Turtles

The family Chelydridae contains three species, which are found only in the Western Hemisphere. Snapping Turtles are large, with long tails, large heads, and relatively small shells. They spend most of their lives in water, seldom emerging to bask, and only occasionally travelling overland. Females move onto land to deposit their eggs. Snapping Turtles are the only species of Chelydridae found in Ontario. They are well known for their aggressive behaviour when encountered out of water.

SNAPPING TURTLE *Chelydra serpentina*

45 cm / 18"

The Snapping Turtle is one of our more common turtle species, although because it seldom leaves water it is not often encountered.

APPEARANCE: The Snapping Turtle is Ontario's largest turtle species. The carapace has three prominent longitudinal ridges, and the rear edge is serrated (upper photo). The plastron is reduced to a small cross-shaped structure, so that the turtle appears to be too big for its shell (middle photo). The tail is long and has a series of bony plates that give it a saw-toothed appearance in profile. The neck is long and the head is large, with powerful jaw muscles. The colour is dark green or black, with a lighter-coloured underside.

▶ The Snapping Turtle can be distinguished from other species by its large size, long neck and tail, and relatively small shell (see Comparative Photographs, pp. 28–29).

HABITAT AND BEHAVIOUR: Snapping Turtles bask much less frequently than most turtle species. Although females may travel extensively to deposit their eggs (lower photo), Snapping Turtles otherwise leave the water infrequently. As a result their shells are often covered in algae. They are usually found in large bodies of water but sometimes inhabit small ponds, where the presence of a large turtle would not be expected. They are poor swimmers, preferring to walk on the bottom. Snapping Turtles have a reputation for aggressive behaviour, and they will attempt to bite if disturbed on land, although they are much less aggressive in water. They are usually scavengers, feeding primarily on carrion, although prey is sometimes captured live. Aquatic vegetation forms a portion of their diet.

REPRODUCTION: The eggs of Snapping Turtles are spherical, about the size of Ping-Pong balls, and thus can be distinguished from the oval eggs of all other Ontario turtle species. A female can produce up to 40 eggs. The eggs are deposited in June and hatch in late August or September. Often the young turtles leave the nest at the same time, creating quite a sight as they head for water.

STATUS: COSEWIC: Not at risk. OMNR: Not at risk.

KINOSTERNIDAE
Musk and Mud Turtles

This family contains 22 species, most in North America, with a few species in Central and South America. Only one species, the Stinkpot, is found in Ontario. Turtles of this family have a hinged plastron, which allows the shell to be partially closed. The shell is more elongate than in most other turtle families, and the carapace is dome-shaped. These turtles seldom leave the water and therefore are not readily seen. Their eggs are elongate and have hard shells, unlike the leathery shells of most turtle eggs.

STINKPOT *Sternotherus odoratus*

13 cm / 5"

Stinkpots are not often seen, because they seldom leave water. Their numbers can be surprisingly high in a suitable habitat.

APPEARANCE: The Stinkpot can be recognized by the narrow domed shape of its shell, which is narrower than that of any other Ontario turtle species. The carapace is brown with black flecks (upper photo) and the plastron is black and yellow (middle photo). The head, limbs, and tail are dark; the head has two light stripes on each side (lower photo). This species is unusual in that some of the scutes of the plastron are not in contact but are separated by skin. The anterior, or front, part of the plastron is movable, allowing the turtle to close its shell partially. In males the plastron is concave and the tail tip is sharply pointed. Stinkpots get their name from the musky smell they may produce when handled.

▶ This species can be distinguished by its domed elongate shell and striped head. Although some other Ontario species have domed shells, only the Stinkpot has a relatively narrow, elongate shell shape (see Comparative Photographs, pp. 28–29).

HABITAT AND BEHAVIOUR: Stinkpots are found in shallow, slow-moving water, usually in lakes or marshes. They are not fast swimmers and usually walk along the bottom. They seldom leave the water even to bask, usually warming themselves in the shallows at the water's edge. Food preferences consist of aquatic insects, crustaceans, molluscs, and carrion.

REPRODUCTION: Females produce two to five eggs. The eggs are elongate and hard-shelled, unlike the eggs of any other Ontario reptile species. Most females dig a hole for the eggs, but some deposit them in leaf litter in sheltered areas, such as under logs or in piles of dead vegetation. Muskrat houses are the preferred nesting location, so females do not need to travel extensively on land to lay their eggs.

STATUS: COSEWIC: Not at risk.
OMNR: Not at risk.

EMYDIDAE
Pond and Marsh Turtles

This is the largest and most widely distributed turtle family, containing 90 species and found on all continents except Australia. Most members of this family are aquatic, although some species spend most of their time on land. These turtles can be found in small ponds, rivers, marshes, and large lakes. All are able to pull in their head and limbs completely, and some species can close the shell partially or completely. Five species of Emydidae occur in Ontario.

PAINTED TURTLE *Chrysemys picta*

Midland 15 cm / 6"   Western 25 cm / 10"

In Ontario there are two subspecies of Painted Turtle. In suitable habitat, Painted Turtles can be very numerous.

APPEARANCE: The two Ontario subspecies of Painted Turtle differ in range, size, and appearance. The Midland Painted Turtle (*Chrysemys picta marginata*) occurs in eastern and southern Ontario. Its carapace and skin are dark green or black, extensively marked with yellow, orange, or red (upper photo). The plastron is yellow, with a dark central marking (middle photo). The usual maximum shell length is 15 cm (6"). The larger Western Painted Turtle (*Chrysemys picta bellii*) is found north and west of Lake Superior. This subspecies can attain a maximum length of 25 cm (10"). Its carapace is usually green, with red or orange markings, and the plastron is yellow or orange with a large irregular dark figure that may cover more than half of the total plastron area (lower photo). In both subspecies females are larger than males. In males the foreclaws are longer than the hindclaws, while in females the claws are approximately the same length. The rear margin of the carapace is smooth, not serrated.

▶ Northern Map Turtles have an unmarked yellow plastron, serrated rear shell margin, and no reddish or orange markings. Spotted Turtles are black with yellow spots (see Comparative Photographs, pp. 28–29).

HABITAT AND BEHAVIOUR: The Painted Turtle is the most widespread turtle species in Ontario and is the species most commonly encountered. Turtles are often seen out of water, basking on almost any available surface. They prefer smaller bodies of water, such as ponds or streams, but may be found in sheltered areas of rivers and lakes. Food consists of aquatic insects and vegetation.

REPRODUCTION: Painted Turtles lay from 4 to 23 eggs, depending on the size of the female. Often several females will construct nests close to one another. If the eggs in these nests are eaten by predators, the area will be littered with eggshells. Young Painted Turtles usually spend the winter in the nest and emerge the following spring.

STATUS: COSEWIC: Not at risk. OMNR: Not at risk.

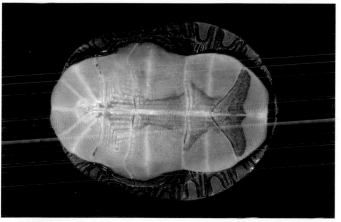

NORTHERN MAP TURTLE *Graptemys geographica*

Female 27 cm / 11"   Male 13 cm / 5"

Northern Map Turtles are normally found only in larger water bodies. The size difference between males and females can make identification confusing.

APPEARANCE: The carapace and skin of Northern Map Turtles are dark green. The head and limbs are covered with yellow stripes and spots (upper photo). The carapace has a serrated rear margin and numerous irregular yellow or light brown markings that suggest a contour map (middle photo). The plastron is yellow with no pattern (lower photo). In smaller individuals the scutes along the dorsal midline are slightly pointed at the rear, giving the turtles a "sawback" appearance. Females are much larger than males, growing up to 27 cm (11") in shell length, while males reach only 13 cm (5"). In males, the claws of the forefeet are longer than the claws of the hindfeet, but in females the claws are the same length. Because they feed on molluscs, female Northern Map Turtles have large jaws and powerful jaw muscles, giving their heads a proportionally larger appearance than those of many other turtle species.

▶ Painted Turtles have a dark pattern on the plastron, a smooth shell margin, and usually some red or orange shell markings. Spotted Turtles are black with obvious yellow spots (see Comparative Photographs, pp. 28–29).

HABITAT AND BEHAVIOUR: Northern Map Turtles prefer large bodies of water and may swim long distances over the course of a summer. They can often be seen basking on logs or rocks near the water's edge. Females feed primarily on molluscs, while males and juveniles consume insects, crayfish, and carrion. Northern Map Turtles overwinter on the bottom of a lake or river. Adults often congregate to hibernate and may travel a considerable distance to the overwintering site.

REPRODUCTION: Eggs are laid in June, at which time females leave the water to search for nesting sites. They may travel some distance from water to nest, although usually not as far as Snapping Turtles. The number of eggs is typically 10–12. The eggs hatch in September, leaving the young turtles only a short time to feed and store reserves before winter.

STATUS: COSEWIC: Not at risk. OMNR: Not at risk.

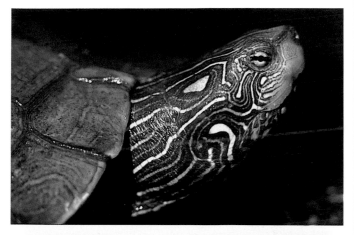

113

BLANDING'S TURTLE *Emydoidea blandingii*

20 cm / 8"

Blanding's Turtles have a high-domed shell. Species with shells of this shape are usually not good swimmers.

APPEARANCE: This turtle is easily recognizable by the domed shape of the shell. In adult Blanding's Turtles the shell is relatively longer and narrower than in most other species, although juveniles have broader, more flattened shells. The carapace is black with numerous small yellow flecks (upper photo). The head and limbs are dark and unmarked, but the underside of the head and neck are bright yellow (middle photo). The neck is relatively long. The plastron is yellow with black patches in adults (lower photo) and almost completely black in juveniles. The plastron is flexible, allowing the shell to be partially closed. In males the plastron is concave, while in females it is flat or slightly convex.

▶ Stinkpots have an elongate domed shell, but without yellow flecks on the shell or a yellow chin. Wood Turtles have a rough shell surface (see Comparative Photographs, pp. 28–29).

HABITAT AND BEHAVIOUR: Blanding's Turtles live in shallow water, usually in large marshes, shallow lakes, and similar bodies of water. They are rather poor swimmers and often move about by walking on the bottom. They feed on aquatic insects, molluscs, crustaceans, and vegetation. They may wander on land, although they usually do not travel far from water except to nest. Blanding's Turtles overwinter at the bottom of water bodies.

REPRODUCTION: Eggs are laid in early summer, and females may travel considerable distances to nest. Between 6 and 11 eggs are produced. The young turtles hatch in late summer and move to water. Young Blanding's Turtles are seldom seen, possibly because they spend their time among thick vegetation at the water's edge.

STATUS: COSEWIC: Not at risk.
OMNR: Not at risk.

SPOTTED TURTLE *Clemmys guttata*

12 cm / 6"

Although they can be abundant in suitable habitat, Spotted Turtles are not frequently observed outside the nesting season. They are one of the first turtle species to become active in early summer.

APPEARANCE: The Spotted Turtle is the smallest Ontario turtle species. Spotted Turtles are black with distinct round yellow spots on the carapace and limbs (upper and middle photos). The plastron may be almost completely black (lower photo), or it may be yellow with black patches, similar to the Wood Turtle. The plastron may be yellow with black patches or may be almost completely black (lower photo). In males the jaws are dark (upper photo), while in females they are lighter, usually yellowish (lower photo). In males the claws of the forefeet are longer than those of the hindfeet, while in females the fore- and hindclaws are the same length.

▶ Painted Turtles have a greenish shell without yellow spots and a yellow plastron with a dark central mark. Northern Map Turtles have a serrated shell margin and a plain yellow plastron. Wood Turtles have a sculpted carapace (see Comparative Photographs, pp. 28–29; see also pp. 118–19).

HABITAT AND BEHAVIOUR: Spotted Turtles prefer smaller, shallow bodies of water such as ponds or marshes. They are quite active in spring and early summer, but their activity decreases as the summer progresses, and they are not usually seen after nesting season. Food consists of aquatic insects, crustaceans, and worms. Winter is spent at the bottom of the home pond.

REPRODUCTION: Nesting occurs in mid-June. Females usually excavate a nest cavity close to water and deposit three to five eggs. Young Spotted Turtles emerge in late summer.

STATUS: COSEWIC: Vulnerable/ special concern. OMNR: Vulnerable.

WOOD TURTLE *Clemmys insculpta*

22 cm / 8.5"

Wood Turtles differ from most Ontario turtle species in that they spend much of their time out of water and feed mostly on vegetation.

APPEARANCE: The shell of the Wood Turtle has a sculpted appearance, unlike the smooth shell of most Ontario turtles (upper photo). The scutes have prominent growth rings, giving them a somewhat pyramidal shape. The carapace, head, and limbs are brown, and the skin has a red or orange wash, especially on the neck and upper limbs (middle photo). The plastron is yellow with black patches (lower photo).

▶ The only other native turtle species with a sculpted carapace is the Snapping Turtle, which is much more aquatic. Blanding's Turtles and Spotted Turtles may have similar plastral markings, but both have smooth shells (see Comparative Photographs, pp. 28–29).

HABITAT AND BEHAVIOUR: Wood Turtles are the most terrestrial of Ontario's native turtles. Although they are usually found in streams or rivers, they may often be found in wooded areas or meadows. They even occasionally hibernate on land, buried in the soil, although they usually overwinter at the bottom of a stream or small river. Young Wood Turtles are more aquatic than adults, seldom leaving shallow water at the edges of marshes or streams. While most Ontario turtle species are principally carnivorous, with plant material making up a small portion of their diet, Wood Turtles primarily consume vegetation. They feed mostly on berries and leaves, although some insects and worms are also eaten. Unlike most turtle species, Wood Turtles do most of their feeding out of water.

REPRODUCTION: Female Wood Turtles dig a nest in a sunny location in late June, usually not far from water. A clutch of 4–13 eggs is produced. The juveniles hatch in late summer and move to suitable aquatic habitat.

STATUS: COSEWIC: Vulnerable/ special concern. OMNR: Vulnerable.

TRIONYCHIDAE
Softshells

The 22 species of softshells occur in North America, Africa, and Asia. Only one species is found in Ontario. As the name implies, the shell is covered with leathery skin rather than hard scutes, although the ribs still make up the shell support structure. The snout is usually elongate. Softshells are fast swimmers and able to move rapidly when on land.

SPINY SOFTSHELL *Apalone spinifera*

42 cm / 16"

This large distinctive turtle is Ontario's only species of softshell.

APPEARANCE: Spiny Softshells are easily recognized by the leathery shell covering, long neck, and long pointed snout. They are one of our largest turtle species. The carapace is grey or brown. In juveniles and adult males, the carapace has light spots with a dark outline (upper photo); the shells of adult females have blurry spots. The name Spiny Softshell comes from the row of short spines along the front edge of the carapace. Males may have similar spines scattered over the surface of the carapace. The plastron is quite small and yellow in colour. Light stripes are present on the sides of the head (middle photo).

▶ This species can be easily distinguished by the combination of long snout, leathery shell, and grey/brown colour. All other Ontario turtles have shorter snouts and their shells are covered in scutes (see Comparative Photographs, pp. 28–29).

HABITAT AND BEHAVIOUR: Spiny Softshells are very good swimmers. They are also able to move very quickly on land and will seek refuge in water if surprised. They can be very aggressive if handled. Often they lie in shallow water with only their nostrils exposed (lower photo). Although they can move considerable distances over the course of a summer, they seldom travel far from water. Food consists of molluscs, crustaceans, and fish. In Ontario, Spiny Softshells occur only in parts of Lake Erie and the Thames River in the southwest, and in the Ottawa River in the east.

REPRODUCTION: Mating occurs in early summer and eggs are deposited in June. Females usually excavate a nest hole close to water and deposit 10 to 30 eggs. The eggs hatch in late summer and the young turtles enter the water immediately.

STATUS: COSEWIC: Threatened.
OMNR: Threatened.

LIZARDS

SCINCIDAE
Skinks

The lizard family Scincidae has a worldwide distribution and contains more than 600 species. Skinks occur in a variety of habitats, from jungles to deserts. Most skinks are insectivorous, but some large Australian species are herbivorous. Their scales are usually large, smooth, and, unlike many lizards, uniform in size and shape all over the body. Ontario has only one species of skink.

COMMON FIVE-LINED SKINK *Eumeces fasciatus*

20 cm / 8"

We are fortunate to have a species of lizard as part of the wildlife of Ontario.

APPEARANCE: Common Five-lined Skinks are black or grey with five white or yellow stripes along the back (upper photo). The colour pattern diminishes with age as the stripes darken, resulting in a less contrasting adult pattern (middle photo). Juveniles have bright blue tails (lower photo), but this colour also fades with age. In adults the tail is grey.

▶ As this is Ontario's only lizard species, identification should be simple, but the Common Five-lined Skink can sometimes be confused with large salamanders. Salamanders have no scales, while skinks, like all lizards, have scaly skin. Salamanders are also much more slow-moving than the fast, agile skinks, and prefer moist habitats, while skinks seek warmer, drier locations.

HABITAT AND BEHAVIOUR: Skinks are active during the day, when they forage for food. Their movement can be quite rapid, and it is often difficult to see skinks as they run quickly through leaf litter. They usually prefer wooded locations with sandy soil and ground cover but also frequent rocky habitat with crevices for concealment. Lizards like to bask, and they can often be seen in sunny locations. They feed on insects, worms, or other invertebrates and can be quite acrobatic in chasing prey. Skinks hibernate in fissures among rocks or buried in the soil.

REPRODUCTION: Egg-laying usually takes place in June. Females produce 6–10 small white eggs, elongate with leathery shells, which are deposited in the shelter of a rock or log. The female will usually guard the eggs until they hatch. The eggs hatch in late summer, and the young skinks are about 5 cm (2") long.

STATUS: COSEWIC: Vulnerable/ special concern. OMNR: Vulnerable.

SNAKES

COLUBRIDAE
Typical Snakes

The Colubridae is the most widely distributed family of snakes. With over 1500 species worldwide, snakes of this family have successfully occupied a variety of habitats. They are found in deserts, in water, in trees, and burrowing underground. Ontario is home to 15 species of snakes, all but one of which belong to the Colubridae.

COMMON GARTERSNAKE *Thamnophis sirtalis*

100 cm / 39"

Although the Common Gartersnake is our most familiar reptile, its variable colours and patterns can lead to mistaken identifications.

APPEARANCE: The maximum length is one metre, but adults do not usually exceed 60 cm (24"). The scales on the back and sides are keeled. The dorsal background colour is black, and the belly is pale yellow or green, sometimes with two rows of dark spots. The light-coloured (usually yellow) stripe on the side is always on the second and third scale rows; this means that there is very little black background visible between the light stripe and the light-coloured belly (upper photo). The mid-dorsal light stripe can be yellow, brown, orange, or even red. Some individuals may have a chequered pattern (middle photo). Some Common Gartersnakes are almost completely black with plain black bellies and white throats (lower photo). Black Common Gartersnakes are usually found only on the shore and islands of Lake Erie.

▶ Eastern Ratsnakes resemble black Common Gartersnakes but have alternating light and dark belly patches and a larger maximum size. Two other striped snake species in southern Ontario, the Eastern Ribbonsnake and Butler's Gartersnake, are more difficult to distinguish from the Common Gartersnake, although they are more slender (see Comparative Photographs, pp. 30–32; see also pp. 132–35).

HABITAT AND BEHAVIOUR: The Common Gartersnake is the most widely distributed snake species in Ontario. The preferred habitat is open areas such as meadows, often in suburban or even urban areas. Gartersnakes readily enter water to feed or to escape predators. They eat insects, worms, small frogs, and fish. When handled, this species may bite and release musk from glands at the base of the tail. Common Gartersnakes hibernate underground, and large numbers may overwinter together in suitable locations.

REPRODUCTION: Common Gartersnakes do not lay eggs but bear their young live. Mating occurs as soon as the snakes emerge from hibernation. Females seek out sunny locations to raise their body temperature and speed embryonic development. The young are born in July.

STATUS: COSEWIC: Not at risk. OMNR: Not at risk.

EASTERN RIBBONSNAKE *Thamnophis sauritus*

100 cm / 36"

Eastern Ribbonsnakes resemble Common Gartersnakes, but they are much more slender. They are not as widely distributed as the Common Gartersnake.

APPEARANCE: Eastern Ribbonsnakes are slender and can be up to one metre in total length, although most individuals are smaller. The tail is proportionally longer than in most other snake species (upper photo). The light stripe on the side is on the third and fourth scale rows, so a black line is present between the light-coloured belly and the light side stripe (middle photo). In Eastern Ribbonsnakes there is a sharp boundary between the light-coloured lips and the dark upper part of the head; in Common Gartersnakes this boundary is blurred and less sharply defined. The chin is light-coloured and there is a yellow or white spot in front of the eye (lower photo). The scales of the back and sides are keeled.

▶ In Common Gartersnakes the light stripe is on the second and third scale rows. In Butler's Gartersnakes the light stripe is on the third scale row, extending somewhat onto the second and fourth rows (see Comparative Photographs, pp. 30–32; see also pp. 130–31, 134–35).

HABITAT AND BEHAVIOUR: Eastern Ribbonsnakes prefer meadows or forest edges, and they are often found near the edges of permanent bodies of water such as marshes, ponds, lakes, and rivers. They will readily enter the water and may be seen basking on offshore rocks or logs. They often feed in water, capturing frogs and fish, although they also eat insects, worms, and other invertebrates. They are much less widely distributed than the Common Gartersnake.

REPRODUCTION: Like their Common Gartersnake relative, Eastern Ribbonsnakes also give birth to live young. Mating occurs in spring, and the young are born in midsummer. The brood size is typically from 5 to 20.

STATUS: COSEWIC: Not at risk. OMNR: Not at risk.

BUTLER'S GARTERSNAKE *Thamnophis butleri*

70 cm / 28"

Butler's Gartersnake has a very limited distribution in Ontario. Its striped pattern may cause it to be confused with other striped species that occur in the same region.

APPEARANCE: The background colour is brown, olive, or black, and the dorsal and lateral stripes can be yellow or orange (upper and middle photos). The belly is light-coloured, usually yellow. The lateral stripe is centred on the third scale row and covers half of the second and fourth rows, so that a dark line is visible between the lateral stripe and the belly scales. A light-coloured spot may be present in front of the eye. The scales of the back and sides are keeled. The head of the Butler's Gartersnake is proportionally much smaller than that of other similar species (lower photo). All-black individuals are known to occur, although less frequently than in Common Gartersnakes.

▶ Eastern Ribbonsnakes are similar in size and general appearance, but the lateral light stripe is on the third and fourth scale rows only. Common Gartersnakes can attain a larger size, and the stripe is on the second and third scale rows (see Comparative Photographs, pp. 30–32; see also pp. 130–33).

HABITAT AND BEHAVIOUR: This species occurs primarily in extreme southwestern Ontario, where it is found in former prairie areas, often in or near wetlands. There are also isolated populations farther north. Meadows and open areas are the preferred habitat. Butler's Gartersnakes are secretive; they are usually found concealed under stones and other shelter. Food consists of small insects, worms, and other invertebrates. Like other snake species, they tend to congregate in overwintering dens.

REPRODUCTION: Mating occurs soon after emergence from overwintering sites. The young are born live, in late July or early August, and usually number between 8 and 15.

STATUS: COSEWIC: Threatened. OMNR: Vulnerable.

NORTHERN WATERSNAKE *Nerodia sipedon*

135 cm / 53"

Northern Watersnakes may be commonly observed in or near aquatic habitats. Their variable colour pattern may result in their being confused with other blotched-pattern snake species.

APPEARANCE: Northern Watersnakes are relatively large, with keeled scales and a blotched colour pattern. The background colour is grey or brown with darker blotches or transverse bands (upper photo). The contrasting markings are much more evident in younger snakes (middle photo); in older snakes the colour pattern may exhibit less contrast. The belly scales have half-moon-shaped markings. Scales of the back and sides are keeled. The Northern Watersnakes found on islands in Lake Erie have a colour pattern in which the darker bands are much less obvious (lower photo), although they are still distinct in juveniles. Some sources consider the Lake Erie Watersnake to be a distinct subspecies.

▶ Northern Watersnakes may be confused with Eastern Racers or Eastern Ratsnakes where their ranges overlap. Racers have smooth scales and adults are unicoloured. Eastern Ratsnakes are glossy black rather than grey or brown (see Comparative Photographs, pp. 30–32).

HABITAT AND BEHAVIOUR: Northern Watersnakes are usually found in or near water. They are less wary of humans than are many other snake species and will often approach swimmers. Northern Watersnakes are normally not aggressive, but they will bite if handled or disturbed, although they are not venomous. They feed on frogs or fish. Like other snake species, Northern Watersnakes overwinter in underground dens.

REPRODUCTION: The Northern Watersnake is viviparous like its close relative the Common Gartersnake. Mating occurs in spring and the young are born in midsummer. Brood sizes range from 10 to 20.

STATUS: COSEWIC: Not at risk. OMNR: Not at risk. Note that both COSEWIC and OMNR have designated the Lake Erie Watersnake as endangered.

137

QUEEN SNAKE *Regina septemvittata*
90 cm / 35"

Queen Snakes are related to Northern Watersnakes, although their colour pattern is quite different. They live in and near streams and are seldom abundant.

APPEARANCE: This species is smaller than its relative the Northern Watersnake, reaching only 90 cm (35") in length, although individuals over 60 cm (24") long are seldom encountered. The colour pattern consists of longitudinal stripes rather than transverse bands. The background colour is medium to dark brown; there is a light stripe along each side and three dark stripes along the back (photos). In some older individuals the dark stripes may not contrast with the background colour. The upper part of the head is brown; the throat, chin, and lips are yellow. The belly is yellow with four dark stripes. The scales on the back and sides are keeled.

▶ Although Queen Snakes resemble Gartersnakes in having light lateral stripes, Gartersnakes also have a stripe down the middle of the back. Red-bellied Snakes and Brownsnakes have a brown background colour, but they do not have lateral light stripes (see Comparative Photographs, pp. 30–32).

HABITAT AND BEHAVIOUR: Queen Snakes are found only in south-western Ontario, where they live along the edges of streams and smaller rivers. They can be found under rocks at the water's edge or in shallow water. They feed on aquatic invertebrates, particularly soft-bodied crayfish that have recently moulted. Queen Snakes seldom venture far from water and can be found by searching under rocks at the water's edge or in shallow water. They are active mostly at night, so they are seldom seen without searching.

REPRODUCTION: Queen Snakes are viviparous like their close relatives the Northern Watersnake and Common Gartersnake. The young are born in late summer and usually number between 7 and 15.

STATUS: COSEWIC: Threatened.
OMNR: Threatened

DEKAY'S BROWNSNAKE *Storeria dekayi*

52 cm / 20"

Although DeKay's Brownsnakes may be common and abundant, even in disturbed areas, they are not often encountered because of their small size and retiring habits.

APPEARANCE: The back has a medium brown background, with two rows of dark spots. In some individuals, these spots may be connected, giving the appearance of dark bands across the back. Down the middle of the back, between the rows of spots, the background colour may be lighter than on the sides, giving the appearance of a broad light stripe (upper photo). There is a dark oblique band on the side of the head behind the eye, and another just below the eye (middle photo). The belly is light-coloured, sometimes with a brown, yellow, or pink wash. The scales on the back and sides are keeled. The young resemble adults, but they have a more contrasting colour pattern as well as prominent light-coloured marks around the neck (lower photo).

▶ Red-bellied Snakes have a similar dorsal colour pattern, but they have a distinctive red belly. Ring-necked Snakes have a bright yellow belly (see Comparative Photographs, pp. 30–32).

HABITAT AND BEHAVIOUR: DeKay's Brownsnakes are often found in or near human habitation, in suburban or even urban areas if suitable habitat is available. Because of their small size, colour, and secretive habits, however, they are not often seen. They can be found in leaf litter, under logs or stones, or burrowing in the soil. In built-up areas they hide under discarded boards or other litter. They feed on a variety of small invertebrates such as insects, earthworms, and slugs. Winter is spent underground.

REPRODUCTION: Mating occurs in spring, soon after the snakes become active. Young are born live, usually in July. Litter size is normally between 7 and 15.

STATUS: COSEWIC: Not at risk.
OMNR: Not at risk.

RED-BELLIED SNAKE *Storeria occipitomaculata*

40 cm / 16"

The distinctive red belly makes this species easy to identify, although its behaviour is secretive, and its brown back provides concealment in the snake's forest-floor habitat.

APPEARANCE: This species can be easily distinguished by its belly colour, which is usually red, sometimes shading to pink or orange (upper photo). The throat is white. Otherwise, in both size and dorsal colour pattern, the Red-bellied Snake resembles its close relative, the DeKay's Brownsnake, and a brief glance may not be sufficient to tell the two species apart. The dorsal colour is brown, sometimes shading to red or grey, with a dark stripe low on each side and two other dark stripes along the back (middle photo). The scales are keeled. Red-bellied Snakes often have three light spots on the back and sides of the neck (lower photo). In young individuals these spots are more prominent and may join together to form a light-coloured neck ring.

▶ DeKay's Brownsnakes have a light brown belly. Ring-necked Snakes have a yellow belly (see Comparative Photographs, pp. 30–32).

HABITAT AND BEHAVIOUR: Red-bellied Snakes can be found among leaf litter on the forest floor, under shelter such as stones, fallen logs, or other debris. They may also be found burrowing in the soil. It is not unusual for them to occur in urban and suburban areas, where they are often found under discarded lumber or other litter Food consists of small invertebrates such as insects, earthworms, and slugs. Like other snake species, they tend to congregate in overwintering dens.

REPRODUCTION: Red-bellied Snakes mate in early spring, as soon as they emerge from their over-wintering sites. They bear live young, numbering between 4 and 13, usually in July.

STATUS: COSEWIC: Not at risk. OMNR: Not at risk.

SMOOTH GREENSNAKE *Opheodrys vernalis*

65 cm / 26"

The distinctive colour of Smooth Greensnakes makes them easy to identify, but also affords them ideal camouflage in their grassy habitat.

APPEARANCE: This species is readily identified by its distinctive green colour (upper and middle photos). The belly and upper lip are white or pale yellow (lower photo). Juveniles are darker than adults, usually olive or bluish-grey. Newly hatched snakes are dark grey, but after about one week they attain the blue-grey juvenile colour. As the snakes grow, the colour gradually changes to green. The scales of the back and sides are smooth.

► Juvenile Eastern Racers are bluish-grey but have a banded colour pattern. Ring-necked Snakes are also bluish-grey, but they have a light-coloured ring around the neck. No other small Ontario snake is green (see Comparative Photographs, pp. 30–32).

HABITAT AND BEHAVIOUR: Smooth Greensnakes prefer grassy areas such as meadows or clearings, where their namesake colour offers camouflage. They often climb into bushes or shrubs, and even move their body slightly to simulate the action of the wind. Food consists of insects, spiders, and snails.

REPRODUCTION: Female Smooth Greensnakes do not deposit their eggs as soon as they are fully formed but instead retain them for a few weeks. As the female basks in the sun, embryonic growth is accelerated and the embryonic period is consequently shortened. When the eggs are eventually laid, in late July or early August, they hatch fairly quickly, normally within two weeks. This allows the newborn snakes more time to feed before the onset of cold weather. The usual number of eggs ranges from 3 to 12.

STATUS: COSEWIC: Not at risk.
OMNR: Not at risk.

RING-NECKED SNAKE *Diadophis punctatus*

60 cm / 24"

The Ring-necked Snake is a secretive woodland species, although it may be abundant in suitable habitat.

APPEARANCE: This small snake species has a plain bluish or grey back with a distinct yellow band on the neck (upper photo). This neck ring is continuous with the yellow belly and upper lip (middle photo). The edges of the yellow belly scales are dark, and there is usually a row of small dark spots down the middle of the belly (lower photo). Scales of the back and sides are smooth.

▶ Young Ring-necked Snakes may be confused with young DeKay's Brownsnakes or Red-bellied Snakes, which also have a ring-like neck marking. These three species may be distinguished by their belly colour. Juvenile Smooth Greensnakes are also bluish-grey, but they lack the yellow neck ring (see Comparative Photographs, pp. 30–32).

HABITAT AND BEHAVIOUR: This species prefers woodland habitat and is most frequently seen in damp areas near the edges of forests. Ring-necked Snakes are secretive, spending the day concealed under cover, and are usually active at night. During hot weather they may spend long periods underground. In most parts of their range Ring-necked Snakes are not common, but they may be locally abundant in some locations. They seem to prefer areas with shallow soil where the bedrock is at or near the surface. They feed mostly on salamanders, especially Red-backed Salamanders, but worms, frogs, and even smaller snakes are also consumed.

REPRODUCTION: The eggs are elongate in shape, two to six in number, and are deposited under logs or in damp leaf litter. They hatch after about two months.

STATUS: COSEWIC: Not at risk. OMNR: Not at risk.

EASTERN HOG-NOSED SNAKE
Heterodon platirhinos
110 cm / 43"

The Eastern Hog-nosed Snake's defensive tactics are an interesting example of reptile behaviour.

APPEARANCE: The distinguishing feature of the Eastern Hog-nosed Snake is the upturned tip of its snout, which gives the snake its name. The colour pattern consists of a light background with dark blotches down the back, and with smaller dark blotches along the sides (upper photo). There is a large dark patch on each side of the head behind the eye. The blotches on the back and sides may be indistinct, but the large head patches are always present (middle photo). The belly is mottled with dark patches on a white background, but the underside of the tail is unmarked white (lower photo). The scales of the back and sides are keeled. Eastern Hog-nosed Snakes can grow to more than a metre in length.

▶ Eastern Hog-nosed Snakes may be confused with other species that have a blotched colour pattern but can be identified by the upturned snout and the dark patches behind the eye (see Comparative Photographs, pp. 30–32).

HABITAT AND BEHAVIOUR: Eastern Hog-nosed Snakes are usually found in areas with sandy soil, in wooded areas, or meadows. They feed almost exclusively on toads. They have two interesting defensive behaviours: first, they will spread the neck (middle photo) and hiss, probably in an attempt to frighten the intruder. If the threat persists, the snake will then "play dead" by turning belly-up (lower photo). Even if the snake is turned right side up, it will turn itself over again. Because of the first behaviour, Hog-nosed Snakes are sometimes mistaken for "cobras" or "puff adders" and killed.

REPRODUCTION: Eggs are laid in a sheltered location, under a log or in leaf litter, in midsummer. The eggs usually number between 10 and 18 and hatch after about two months.

STATUS: COSEWIC: Threatened.
OMNR: Vulnerable.

MILKSNAKE *Lampropeltis triangulum*
90 cm / 35"

Milksnakes can often be found near human habitation. In some cases their slight resemblance to rattlesnakes provokes an antagonistic human response.

APPEARANCE: The background colour is grey, or brownish-grey, with reddish blotches outlined in black (upper photo). There is a series of large blotches along the back, alternating with much smaller blotches low on the sides. The head bears a V- or Y-shaped light mark (middle photo). The belly is chequered black on a white background. The young have a similar colour pattern to the adults but are more brightly coloured (upper photo). The scales on the back and sides are smooth.

▶ No other blotched snake species has red colouring and a Y-shaped mark on the head (see Comparative Photographs, pp. 30–32).

HABITAT AND BEHAVIOUR: Preferred habitat is open forest, forest edges, meadows, and cultivated areas. Milksnakes can be found in leaf litter or under debris. They overwinter underground in rock formations and may enter buildings through unsuspected openings in foundations. Milksnakes are constrictors and feed on rodents, frogs, birds, and other snakes. Their preference for mice often attracts them to barns or other buildings. Their name derives from the old folklore that they milk cows. Milksnakes are aggressive and may bite if handled, although they are not venomous. They also vibrate the tail tip if agitated. This habit has led to the death of many Milksnakes at the hands of humans who mistake them for rattlesnakes.

REPRODUCTION: Milksnakes produce from 6 to 15 elongate eggs (lower photo), which are deposited in sheltered locations such as under logs or in rotting stumps. The eggs hatch after about two months.

STATUS: COSEWIC: Not at risk.
OMNR: Not at risk.

EASTERN FOXSNAKE *Elaphe gloydi*

170 cm / 67"

The Eastern Foxsnake's appetite for rodents and preference for water often brings it into contact with humans, and it may even be found sharing human habitation.

APPEARANCE: The Eastern Foxsnake is a fairly large species with a blotched colour pattern. As in many blotched snakes, a series of large blotches along the back alternates with smaller blotches on the sides. The background colour is yellow or pale brown, and the blotches are darker brown (upper and middle photos). The head is yellow below and reddish brown above, with dark bars between, behind, and below the eyes (lower photo). The belly has alternating yellow and dark brown patches. The scales on the back are keeled, but those on the sides are smooth. The maximum length is 170 cm (67"), although most individuals are smaller. Newborn Eastern Foxsnakes measure about 30 cm (12").

▶ The Eastern Foxsnake is unique among blotched-pattern snakes in having a yellow background colour with dark brown blotches. Young Eastern Foxsnakes have a grey background colour and may be confused with young Milksnakes (see Comparative Photographs, pp. 30–32).

HABITAT AND BEHAVIOUR: Eastern Foxsnakes are usually found near water, and their present distribution is near the shores of lakes Erie and Huron, as well as Georgian Bay. They are not uncommon around buildings, where they search for food. They overwinter underground and may enter houses in the autumn through cracks in the foundation. They eat rodents, birds, and frogs, which they kill by constriction. Eastern Foxsnakes frequently vibrate their tail when alarmed, and this habit, along with their colour pattern, can lead to their being mistaken for rattlesnakes. Eastern Foxsnakes are not aggressive and will rarely bite if handled. They produce a scent similar to that of foxes.

REPRODUCTION: Eggs are laid under cover such as logs or in leaf litter, in midsummer. The eggs usually number 10–20 and hatch after about two months.

STATUS: COSEWIC: Threatened. OMNR: Threatened.

EASTERN RATSNAKE *Elaphe obsoleta*
200 cm / 78"

Although it is rarely seen, Ontario's largest snake presents a striking sight when fully grown.

APPEARANCE: This species can attain a larger maximum size than any other snake species in Ontario. In adults the back is a striking glossy black (upper photo). The backs of young snakes have a pattern of black blotches on a grey background, but the colour darkens and the pattern diminishes as the snakes grow. The underside is white with diffuse mottling and sometimes a black-on-white chequered pattern. The scales on the back are keeled, but those on the sides are smooth. The throat, chin, and upper lip are white (middle photo).

▶ Adults are easily identified by their black colour. Juveniles may resemble Northern Watersnakes but can be distinguished by their white throat, belly pattern, and smoother scales (see Comparative Photographs, pp. 30–32).

HABITAT AND BEHAVIOUR: Eastern Ratsnakes are constrictors and feed mostly on rodents and birds, although frogs and other snakes are also eaten. They sometimes climb into bushes or low trees, searching for bird nests. They prefer wooded areas, although they may be found in fields and meadows. Like some other species of non-venomous snakes, Eastern Ratsnakes shake their tails when agitated. Although they are not normally aggressive, the habit of shaking the tail, combined with their large size, can antagonize humans. This species has an unusual distribution in Ontario, with separate populations in the southwest and at the eastern end of Lake Ontario. It is not known whether Eastern Ratsnakes once occurred to the north of Lake Ontario and were extirpated because of human disturbance, or whether they moved into their present locations independently from the south.

REPRODUCTION: Eastern Ratsnakes produce from 10 to 16 eggs (lower photo), which are deposited in sheltered locations such as under rocks or fallen logs. Eggs are laid in early summer and hatch in late summer. The length of the incubation period depends on temperature.

STATUS: COSEWIC: Threatened. OMNR: Threatened.

EASTERN RACER *Coluber constrictor*

180 cm / 71"

This large, active species is one of Ontario's rarest and most interesting snakes.

APPEARANCE: The Eastern Racer is one of two large snake species in Ontario that does not have a blotched adult colour pattern. Adults are blue, sometimes with a green or grey wash, and the belly is pale blue. The throat, chin, and upper lip are white, and there is a dark bar through the eye (upper and middle photos). Juveniles have dark blotches on the back (lower photo), but these disappear with age. The scales on the back and sides are smooth. The maximum length is about 180 cm (71"), but few individuals attain this size.

▶ On Pelee Island, juvenile Eastern Racers may be confused with Northern Watersnakes, which have keeled scales and a distinctive belly pattern. Juvenile Smooth Greensnakes are also bluish in colour (see Comparative Photographs, pp. 30–32).

HABITAT AND BEHAVIOUR: In Ontario, Eastern Racers are found only on Pelee Island. They prefer open fields or low brush habitat and will readily climb shrubs or low branches. They overwinter below ground in rock formations and sometimes enter buildings. Racers vibrate their tails when excited and are therefore sometimes mistaken for rattlesnakes. Racers are active, fast snakes that find prey by searching rather than lying in wait. They often travel with the head raised high; most other snake species keep the head relatively low. Food consists of frogs, rodents, insects, and small birds. Despite their scientific name, Eastern Racers do not kill their prey by constriction, although they may loop their body over the prey to restrain it until it is swallowed.

REPRODUCTION: Females produce 10–20 eggs, which are deposited in sheltered locations under logs or other debris. The young hatch in late summer.

STATUS: COSEWIC: Endangered.
OMNR: Endangered.

VIPERIDAE
Vipers

Vipers are the most widely distributed family of venomous snakes, with about 200 species in Africa, Europe, Asia, and North and South America. They are characterized by fangs that can be folded back when not in use and extended to inject venom when needed. Rattlesnakes are specialized vipers found in North, Central, and South America; they can be readily identified by the rattle at the tip of the tail. Ontario's only venomous snake, the Massasuaga, is a rattlesnake.

NOTE:

There are few recorded occurrences of bites by venomous snakes in Ontario, and only one reported death. Encounters between humans and Massasaugas do occur, but the snakes usually detect approaching humans and flee beforehand. The snakes take refuge under shelter such as rocks or logs and, if disturbed there, may bite. Care should be taken before picking up anything from the ground within the Massasauga's range. In case of a bite, the victim should be taken to hospital. The location of the bite should be immobilized, but a tourniquet should not be used. Rattlesnake bites are very painful, but on a healthy human the venom is slow-acting. All hospitals in the range of the Massasauga are equipped to handle bites.

MASSASAUGA *Sistrurus catenatus*
100 cm / 30"

Like all venomous snakes, the Massasauga carries an undeserved bad reputation.

APPEARANCE: The back has a grey background with a row of large darker blotches down the centre and smaller blotches along each side (upper and middle photos). A large dark horizontal bar extends backward from the eye (lower photo). The belly is black, often with lighter markings. The tail ends in a distinctive rattle. The scales on the back and sides are keeled. The Massasauga is the only Ontario snake species in which the pupil of the eye is vertical, similar to that of a cat.

▶ Several other snake species have blotched colour patterns, but the Massasauga can be distinguished by its black belly and the rattle on its tail, which is usually obvious (see Comparative Photographs, pp. 30–32).

HABITAT AND BEHAVIOUR: This member of the rattlesnake group is Ontario's only venomous reptile. Human activities such as agriculture and construction have reduced the range of the Massasauga, along with that of other snake species. Formerly widely distributed in southwestern Ontario, it is now found only in rocky and scrub habitat near the shores of lakes Erie and Huron, and Georgian Bay. Massasaugas obtain food by lying in wait for prey. The venom from their bites immobilizes prey, and they are thus able to capture comparatively large prey animals. They feed at night, usually on rodents. All rattlesnakes have heat-sensitive pits between the eye and nostril (lower photo) and can thereby detect the presence of warm-bodied prey.

REPRODUCTION: The young are born live and usually number seven or eight. Newborn Massasaugas have a rattle consisting of a single segment, or "button." Another segment is added to the rattle each time the snake sheds its skin. This can happen several times each year, so the number of rattle segments is not a measure of the age of the snake.

STATUS: COSEWIC: Threatened. OMNR: Threatened.

EASTERN BOX TURTLE *Terrapene ornata*
18 cm / 7"

Although they are members of the aquatic turtle family Emydidae,
Box Turtles are terrestrial and seldom enter water. The brightly marked,
high-domed shell is a distinctive identification character. Eastern Box
Turtles have been reported from Point Pelee on Lake Erie and may be
present in nearby locations as well. These turtles are native to the southeastern part of the United States and are often kept as pets. The individuals
reported from Ontario are most likely once-captive animals that have
been released. It is not known whether they can reproduce successfully
in Ontario.

RED-EARED SLIDER *Trachemys scripta*
25 cm / 10"

Red-eared Sliders resemble Painted Turtles, but are easily identified by
the red mark on the side of the head. They also grow larger than most
Painted Turtles, attaining a maximum shell length of 25 cm (10"). Red-
eared Sliders are familiar pet turtles, available in many pet shops. As they
grow larger, many are abandoned into the wild. These turtles are native to
the southeastern United States, and it is not known whether they can
reproduce successfully in Ontario.

TIMBER RATTLESNAKE *Crotalus horridus*
180 cm / 70"

The Timber Rattlesnake has dark bands on a yellowish-brown background,
with a light brown belly. There are historical records of the Timber
Rattlesnake in the Niagara region, but this species has not been reported in
Ontario since the 1940s. It has been designated as extirpated by COSEWIC
and endangered by OMNR.

GLOSSARY

anaerobic metabolism—metabolism carried out in the absence of oxygen.

carapace—the dorsal or upper part of the shell of a turtle.

chromosomes—structures in living cells that carry genetic information, or genes. The cells of most animals have two sets of chromosomes (the diploid, or 2N, number), but some have three sets (triploid, or 3N), four sets (tetraploid, or 4N), or even five sets (pentaploid, or 5N).

cloaca—the chamber into which the digestive, urinary, and reproductive tracts empty. The cloaca opens to the exterior through the anus, or vent.

concave—curving inward.

convex—curving outward.

costal grooves—a series of vertical grooves on the sides of some species of salamanders.

diverse—containing a large number of species.

dorsal—pertaining to the back, or upper side.

gynogenesis—method of reproduction whereby the offspring are genetically identical to their female parent, although sperm from a male is required to initiate growth of the embryo.

herpetofauna—that portion of animal life made up of amphibians and reptiles.

hibernaculum (Pl. -la)—the location at which animals, usually snakes, spend the winter. Hibernacula, or dens, are located underground, below the frost line, usually in rock formations. An ideal hibernaculum provides protection both from predators and below-freezing temperatures. Many snakes can use the same hibernaculum and usually return to it year after year.

hybrid—offspring whose parents belong to different species.

juvenile—a young animal that has the adult body form but is not yet mature.

keeled scales—scales on the back and sides, each having a ridge, or keel, down the centre (see pp. 133, 158, lower photos). In some species the scales are smooth, with no keel (see p. 15, lower photo).

larva—the stage of life before transformation to the adult body form.

metamorphosis—the transformation from larva to adult form.

microhabitat—a small portion of a species' habitat, often used for a specific purpose such as egg-laying or overwintering.

nasolabial groove—a groove running from the nostril to the upper lip in salamanders of the family Plethodontidae.

oviparous—reproducing by laying eggs.

plastron—the lower part of a turtle shell.

protract—to extend (the tongue) outside the mouth, usually to catch prey.

respiration—exchange of oxygen and carbon dioxide, usually through lungs or gills.

scale rows—longitudinal rows in which the scales on the back and sides of snakes are arranged. Scale rows are numbered, beginning from the row that is adjacent to the large belly scales. The number of scale rows is sometimes used to identify snakes.

scutes—large scales on the shell of a turtle.

venter—belly or underside.

ventral—pertaining to the belly, or lower side.

vertebrates—animals that have backbones (fishes, amphibians, reptiles, birds, and mammals).

viviparous—bearing live young, rather than laying eggs.

CHECKLIST OF ONTARIO AMPHIBIANS AND REPTILES

This list contains 53 species of amphibians and reptiles that have been reported from Ontario. Introduced species are indicated by an (I) and extirpated species by an (E).

Amphibians

SALAMANDERS
❑ Mudpuppy
❑ Eastern Newt
❑ Blue-spotted Salamander
❑ Jefferson Salamander
❑ Small-mouthed Salamander
❑ Spotted Salamander
❑ Tiger Salamander (E)
❑ Northern Dusky Salamander
❑ Northern Two-lined Salamander
❑ Four-toed Salamander
❑ Eastern Red-backed Salamander
❑ Spring Salamander (E)
❑ Red Salamander (I)

FROGS AND TOADS
❑ American Toad
❑ Fowler's Toad
❑ Gray Treefrog
❑ Northern Cricket Frog
❑ Spring Peeper
❑ Western Chorus Frog
❑ Boreal Chorus Frog
❑ Wood Frog
❑ Northern Leopard Frog
❑ Pickerel Frog
❑ Green Frog
❑ Mink Frog
❑ American Bullfrog

Reptiles

TURTLES
❑ Snapping Turtle
❑ Stinkpot
❑ Painted Turtle
❑ Northern Map Turtle
❑ Blanding's Turtle
❑ Spotted Turtle
❑ Wood Turtle
❑ Spiny Softshell
❑ Eastern Box Turtle (I)
❑ Red-eared Slider (I)

LIZARDS
❑ Common Five-lined Skink

SNAKES
❑ Common Gartersnake
❑ Eastern Ribbonsnake
❑ Butler's Gartersnake
❑ Northern Watersnake
❑ Queen Snake
❑ DeKay's Brownsnake
❑ Red-bellied Snake
❑ Smooth Greensnake
❑ Ring-necked Snake
❑ Eastern Hog-nosed Snake
❑ Milksnake
❑ Eastern Foxsnake
❑ Eastern Ratsnake
❑ Eastern Racer
❑ Massasauga
❑ Timber Rattlesnake (E)

INDEX

Acris crepitans, 74
Ambystoma
   jeffersonianum, 48
   laterale, 46
   maculatum, 52
   texanum, 50
   tigrinum, 96
Apalone spinifera, 122

Brownsnake, DeKay's, 140
Bufo americanus, 66
   fowleri, 68
Bullfrog, American, 94

Chelydra serpentina, 102
Chrysemys picta, 110
Clemmys guttata, 116
   insculpta, 118
Coluber constrictor, 156
Crotalus horridus, 162

Desmognathus fuscus, 56
Diadophis punctatus, 146

Elaphe gloydi, 152
   obsoleta, 154
Emydoidea blandingii, 116
Eumeces fasciatus, 126
Eurycea bislineata, 58

Foxsnake, Eastern, 152
Frog,
   Boreal Chorus, 80
   Green, 90
   Mink, 92
   Northern Cricket, 74
   Northern Leopard, 86
   Pickerel, 88
   Western Chorus, 78
   Wood, 84
   See also Bullfrog, Peeper,
   and Treefrog.

Gartersnake, Butler's, 134
   Common, 130
Graptemys geographica,
   112
Greensnake, Smooth, 144
Gyrinophilus
   porphyriticus, 96

Hemidactylium scutatum,
   60
Heterodon platirhinos, 148
Hyla versicolor, 72

Lampropeltis triangulum,
   150

Massasauga, 160
Milksnake, 150
Mudpuppy, 38

Necturus maculosus, 38
Nerodia sipedon, 136
Newt, Eastern, 42
Notophthalmus
   viridescens, 42

Opheodrys vernalis, 144

Peeper, Spring, 76
Plethodon cinereus, 62
Pseudacris crucifer, 76
   maculata, 80
   triseriata, 78
Pseudotriton ruber, 96

Racer, Eastern, 156
Rana catesbeiana, 94
   clamitans, 90
   palustris, 88
   pipiens, 86
   septentrionalis, 92
   sylvatica, 84
Ratsnake, Eastern, 154
Rattlesnake, Timber, 162
Regina septemvittata, 138
Ribbonsnake, Eastern, 132

Salamander,
   Blue-spotted, 46
   Eastern Red-backed, 62
   Four-toed, 60
   Jefferson, 48
   Northern Dusky, 56
   Northern Two-lined, 58
   Red, 96
   Small-mouthed, 50
   Spotted, 52
   Spring, 96

   Tiger, 96
Sistrurus catenatus, 160
Skink, Common Five-
   lined, 126
Slider, Red-eared, 162
Snake,
   Eastern Hog-nosed, 148
   Queen, 138
   Red-bellied, 142
   Ring-necked, 146
   See also Brownsnake,
   Foxsnake, Gartersnake,
   Greensnake, Massasauga,
   Milksnake, Racer,
   Ratsnake, Rattlesnake,
   Ribbonsnake, *and*
   Watersnake.
Softshell, Spiny, 122
Sternotherus odoratus, 106
Stinkpot, 106
Storeria dekayi, 140
   occipitomaculata, 142

Terrapene ornata, 162
Thamnophis butleri, 134
   sauritus, 132
   sirtalis, 130
Toad,
   American, 66
   Fowler's, 68
Trachemys scripta, 162
Treefrog, Gray, 72
Turtle,
   Blanding's, 114
   Box, 162
   Northern Map, 112
   Painted, 110
   Snapping, 102
   Spotted, 116
   Wood, 118
   See also Slider,
   Softshell, *and* Stinkpot.

Watersnake, Northern, 136

PHOTO CREDITS

Upper-case letters adjacent to each page number refer to the position of the photograph on the page (U = upper; M = middle; L = lower). Lower case letters (a–g, top to bottom) refer to the position of the photograph on a comparative photographs page.

G. M. Allen, 26b, 28b, 30c, 31f, 31g, 69M, 107U, 123M, 135U, 137L, 139U, 143L, 147U, 147L, 157U

R. Altig, 25b, 26d, 34U, 35U, 43I, 51L, 53M, 57U, 57L, 69L, 75U, 75L, 79L, 85L, 87L, 89L, 93L, 95L

J. Cebek, 119U

W. A. Crich, 28a, 28c, 31e, 98U, 103U, 111U, 145M, 151L

David M. Dennis, 39L, 61L

Mary Ferguson, 26e, 29a, 40, 77M, 85M, 95M, 115U

Jim Flynn, 29d, 120, 123U, 123L, 124

Tom R. Johnson, 73L

James Kamstra, 24b, 24f, 27e, 32d, 36, 39M, 43U, 51U, 53L, 59M, 93U, 104, 107M, 107L, 127U, 127M, 135L, 145L, 153M, 153L, 157L

Albert Kuhnigk, 81L

Jeff LeClere, 103M

Ross MacCulloch, 27b, 27d, 27f, 35L (left), 87U, 91U, 93M, 95U, 111M, 111L, 113L, 115L, 117L, 149M

J. Martinez, 59L, 77L

Robert McCaw, 28d, 30b, 31c, 64, 67M, 70, 82, 91M, 91L, 97, 103L, 108, 113U, 113M, 115M, 128, 133M, 133L, 141U, 141M, 143M, 155M, 161L

John Mitchell, 29b, 32a, 32e, 47U, 61M, 63U, 87M, 117U, 117M, 137U, 137M, 155L, 158, 161M

Robert W. Murphy, 23, 24d, 26c, 47M, 73U, 131M, 157M, 161U

Michael Patrikeev, 25c, 25d, 25e, 30a, 30d, 31b, 31d, 32b, 54, 59U, 61U, 63M, 63L, 73M, 79M, 99, 131U, 139M, 139L, 143U, 145U, 147M, 149U, 149L, 153U, 155U

Peter W. Post, 100, 127L

John Reaume, 3, 31a, 44, 69U, 89M, 98L, 131L, 135M, 141L, 151M

Michael Redmer, 24a, 33, 34L, 39M, 51M, 75M

Royal Ontario Museum, 24c, 24e, 25a, 26a, 26f, 26g, 27a, 27c, 29c, 35L (right), 43M, 49U, 49M, 53U, 57M, 67U, 67L, 77U, 79U, 81U, 81M, 85U, 89U, 119M, 119L, 133U

R. Wayne Van Devender, 47L, 49L

Douglas Wechsler, 32c, 151U

ACKNOWLEDGMENTS

This book follows several excellent previous guides to amphibians and reptiles of Ontario and Canada by Shelley Logier, Francis Cook, and Bob Johnson. I thank the members of the herpetofauna naturalist community who contributed photographs. Thanks are also due to all who participated in the Ontario Herpetofaunal Summary, upon which the distribution maps are based, and to Summary co-ordinators Mike Oldham and Wayne Weller. Francis Cook and Tony Russell contributed useful suggestions toward the writing of the book. Early versions were much improved by science editor Richard Winterbottom, and two anonymous reviewers, and by the publication editors, Glen Ellis, Andrea Gallagher, and Alex Schultz.

My interest in herpetology has been fostered by my parents, who encouraged my raising of tadpoles, by my academic mentors, Drs. J. R. Bider, Macdonald College of McGill University, and D. M. Secoy, University of Regina, and by my colleagues Bob Murphy and Amy Lathrop, Royal Ontario Museum. Virginia Morin and Tara Winterhalt of ROM Publications designed the page layouts, maps, and cover. Glen Ellis oversaw the entire project.

Finally, I thank my wife, Pat, a constant source of inspiration.

Ross D. MacCulloch

The Royal Ontario Museum gratefully acknowledges the Louise Hawley Stone Charitable Trust for its generous support of this publication.

McClelland & Stewart acknowledges the financial support of the Government of Canada through the Book Publishing Industry Development Program for our publishing activities. We further acknowledge the support of the Canada Council for the Arts and the Ontario Arts Council for our publishing program.

Scans by Hume Imaging Inc., Toronto, Ontario.

Printed and bound in Canada by St. Joseph's / M.O.M. Printing, Ottawa, Ontario.

Front Cover: Eft (juvenile) of the Eastern Newt, *Notophthalmus viridescens,* by John Reaume. These brightly coloured salamanders are often encountered in forest-floor habitat. Although both the larvae and adults are aquatic, juvenile newts spend one to three years on land before maturing. Their bright orange-and-red colouring warns of noxious compounds secreted by skin glands.

Back Cover (clockwise from top left): Common Five-lined Skink, Peter W. Post; Painted Turtles, Robert McCaw; Blanding's Turtle, Robert McCaw; Milksnake, Douglas Wechsler; Blue-spotted Salamander, Robert W. Murphy; American Bullfrog, Ross D. MacCulloch; Common Gartersnake, Robert McCaw; Centre: Gray Treefrog, Robert W. Murphy. Author Photo: Amy Lathrop